THE BITTERSWEET SYMPHONY OF LIFE

VAL DOWD

ISBN: 9798590561735

DEDICATION

For our lovely Catherine thanks to whom our family story was made extraordinary and our lives richer.

Bittersweet: Containing a mixture of sadness and happiness

Symphony: A long piece of orchestral music which consists of a changing pattern of movement. Sections usually include fast, slow, energetic, dramatic.

ACKNOWLEDGMENTS

Thank you to all those who read my book and encouraged me to publish, I would never have achieved this without your positive comments!

A special thank you to our son Tom Dowd and my niece Emma Parmar who helped me produce the beautiful cover for my book.

Any profits from this publication will be donated to Naomi House & Jacksplace hospices in Sutton Scotney, England, who provide expert hospice care to local life limited and life threatened children, young adults and their extended families.

CONTENTS

INTRODUCTION

My inspiration for this book is twofold. I started writing my story during carers' week a few years ago, as I empathised with many of the stories told, but did not hear about a parent caring for a child born with disabilities. I completed it during the lockdowns of 2020 as I suddenly found myself needing a constructive way of occupying my leisure time and this became my focus. My other reason for putting pen to paper is more selfish as although this is my story, it is our daughter Catherine's story too, and I want to make sure the experiences we shared as a family, and the strength and beauty that we were privileged to see in our precious little girl are remembered.

I started writing an article and it grew! I have written about the main events which I feel had the most impact on us as a family or me as Catherine's Mum, and they are written from my point of view.

I am aware that every carer's experiences are completely different and therefore all tell a different story. This is mine about Catherine's beautiful but too short life, and her struggle with disability, entwined with my story told from the point of view of being an Occupational Therapist, a mother, and Catherine's main carer.

I know some of the feelings I describe below will have been shared by all my fellow special needs parent carers at some point. Our stories of caring are different in that they begin with a period of grieving, for our child that was expected, with all the hopes, dreams and choices that gradually fade as the extent of our child's disability is realised.

A parent carer will be a carer for the whole of their child's life through to adulthood, although many children with complex health needs do not survive to adulthood and this possibility makes every illness, however minor, exceptionally worrying times. Alternatively, a child who becomes an adult with extra needs may outlive their carer parents, who, then, will look after them when their parents are gone? Either way, nothing prepares you for this hand life has dealt, and how you deal with it is an individual thing and each of our paths is as unique as our child.

Parenting a child with disabilities will completely change your view of the world! Everything must be approached in a different way when you are pushing a wheelchair and seating system containing a child who is not able to help themselves. Everything from access, travel, interaction with others to planning social life, or even just planning your day, provides a huge lesson in learning to be adaptable.

For me, being a therapist, I now understand how totally different it is to be on the receiving end of care and advice rather than giving. My career in Occupational Therapy was at times both helpful and a hinderance but definitely a mixed blessing when it became blended with my role as a carer. I can say that most of the time I felt every bit as inexperienced in looking after our poorly baby as a parent with no health care background.

We are aware that we are fortunate to live in a country where we have the benefit of the NHS and Children's Services to provide specialist support to children like Catherine. My frustration is that these resources do not always reach those who need them. There is no doubt that children with extra needs benefit from being in a joined-up system but it is true that it feels like a series of battles to get the right help in a timely way.

As individuals and as a family we are very different people now, and we are proud that not only did we rise to the challenge of being a special needs family but that we embraced it, and were extremely proud to have had the privilege of looking after our beautiful life limited daughter. Being carers for the 14 years of Catherine's life, taught us to appreciate all that we have, and helped us build a resilience to put other crises in perspective and hopefully take nothing for granted.

1

ME

I am an Occupational Therapist now, although this was not always my career, I was late to the party! I grew up in Southgate in North London suburbia as a very much-loved middle child between my equally loved two brothers in what I consider to be a perfect childhood. My parents both worked in central London, my Mum as a secretary for a Senior Lecturer at the North London Polytechnic (now University of North London) and loved her job. Dad was a hardworking man who worked in printing and although I think he enjoyed the work in the early days, changes in technology meant his job had became more about profit than quality which was not his way. He was a careful and considered man and towards the end of his working life he was very much counting the days to retirement. By this time he was definitely working only for the money he needed to give the best life to his family rather than for the job. Mum and Dad were always encouraging but never pushy parents and always presented a united front. They both retired around the same time although Mum would have been happy to work on, Dad was extremely glad to retire and concentrate on his home and family and growing number of grandchildren.

I left school at 16 with a huge sigh of relief (anyone who tells you your school days are the best of your life is fibbing!) and signed up to our local polytechnic to do combined A levels and Secretarial course. I didn't know what I wanted to do with my career and at that age I was more interested in earning enough money to live independently and save up to travel. The secretarial course and a couple of very average A Levels enabled me to work in London with a salary which allowed me to house share further into the city and to go out with friends most nights. My teens and early 20's were very much about enjoying myself! I jumped around a series of well-paid temporary secretarial jobs which also allowed me to save money to travel.

I had been on a bus trek across the USA with my childhood friend at the age of 19, I am glad that we were brave enough to do that at a young age as it was a wonderful experience. We were too young to drink alcohol in most states, unlike here in the UK when there was no such thing as an ID check back in the day. I had been going to the same North London pub every week for at least a year before I celebrated my 18th birthday there! I bumped into my same friend a couple of years later, on the London underground, and told her how much I wanted to travel again, my next plan was to go to Australia. Without any kind of a pause she said she would come with me and a couple of months later, just after our 21st birthdays, we flew to Sydney and began a year's working holiday. It was an amazing time, Australia is beautiful and we had all kinds of experiences, good, bad, hilarious and embarrassing (you can imagine) it was a very character forming time, and we both fell in love with Australia. We were able to use our secretarial skills to work whilst we were over there, to support our travels and we saw as much of the country as we could in the time.

When we returned to the UK, I continued working as a secretary but began to realise that I wanted a different focus for my working life, the role which had given me so much freedom and money to enjoy myself was leaving me feeling unfulfilled. It was my Mum who read an article about

Occupational Therapy who hit upon the right direction for me.

I liked the idea of using everyday activity to help people achieve their best quality of life and it appeared the profession would offer a wide range of areas in which to work and lead to good career development opportunities. Rehabilitation can be a positive part of a person's illness or disability and the choice of directions to follow as a clinician appealed to me. I applied, and was accepted by Liverpool College of Occupational Therapy, with an offer to start immediately. They had been awarded a sponsorship place at the last minute and were looking for someone who could start straight away (I had actually been applying for the following year). I accepted, handed in my notice on the house I was sharing, the job I was doing and moved to Liverpool two weeks after my offer.

I loved my new venture, Liverpool is a wonderful city to be a student, it's beautiful architecture, historic landmarks and history of music, means there seems to be a place of interest on every corner. They have a choice of unique traditional pubs, great night life and at the time they had recently completed the new shopping centre and Albert Dock area. I embraced the student life and enjoyed my studies and placements which I made sure encompassed as many different disciplines as possible: medical, surgical, neurology, head injuries, burns, and areas of mental health including alcohol & drug rehab, eating disorders, adult and elderly. I moved around the country as much as possible too: Halton Hospital in Runcorn, Birmingham Accident and Selly Oak Hospitals in the Midlands, The German Hospital in London Hackney, Countess of Chester and finally Tone Vale Hospital in Exeter. It was also the first time I had lived anywhere in the UK other than north and east London and I loved learning about the diversity of cultures, and the way accents and colloquialisms change even within a few miles. It was an enriching 3 years in so many ways.

During the second year of my training, which was mostly spent out on placements, my student friend and I went on holiday to Spain, we took £50 for spending money, even 30 years ago this definitely wasn't enough! It was on this holiday to Torremolinos where I met my future husband Tony, who was away with his Basingstoke friends and appeared to be making a comprehensive list of all the different "happy hour" bars, eg two drinks for the price of one, a perfect fit for our low budget! And who says holiday romances don't last?!

Doing my training I had decided I would like to work in mental health and my first role as a qualified OT was working in an adult Assessment Unit. Although it had high success statistics, I felt just reinforced the fact that we cannot offer the right support in our society to prevent the "revolving door" syndrome. This is where people would be admitted with various emergency conditions would then work hard, and with the right professional guidance, find their way back to good mental health. Unfortunately they were then discharged back to the same poor living conditions and lack of purpose, and gradually become ill again. I was working in the Worthing area on the south coast which was one of the conditions of my student sponsorship, I needed to do 2 years in the area, so I finished my Basic Grade rotation and applied for jobs nearer to Basingstoke and my husband to be.

Another move, another town, but this time I loved my job, the switch to working in a busy acute general hospital, and I was happy to stay put. Hampshire is a beautiful county and the Royal Hampshire County Hospital in Winchester where I was working suited me. The OT department were mainly young, single, fun and with forward thinking managers. My role at the hospital was varied and over the time I worked there I was based in clinical areas of medical, surgical, elderly care and orthopaedics. We were mainly involved assessing and treating on the wards and in the OT department, but we also did home assessments when discharge planning for people in more complex situations. There was room to grow in my career and the friends I made here were so like me in outlook and sense of humour, we used to socialise outside of work as well. I have very fond memories of my time in Winchester (and conveniently there was a pub on the hospital site!). It is true that one of the coping mechanisms of health care professionals is to have an alternative sense of humour and I can still laugh when I remember some of the situations we found so funny in those days.

I was ambitious and enjoyed the non-clinical side of being a therapist as well as my clinical work and became Head Occupational Therapist of St Paul's Hospital, a Community hospital for Elderly Care in Winchester, and then also of the Royal Hants County Hospital where I had started my working in Winchester. This was a really enjoyable time of my life, I had a lovely circle of friends locally, I regularly visited Mum and Dad in London and was still in touch with many of my childhood friends who I met up with when I could. Tony is one of four, he has three sisters, and at that time his family and mine were growing with new nieces and nephews, we had just got married and were looking forward to building a life and family together.

2

BABY

Both of our children were planned and very much wanted babies. Our son Thomas bounced into our lives after a trouble-free pregnancy and apart from being an undiagnosed breach (and an emergency caesarean section), his birth was perfect. We were bursting with pride from his first breath. Thomas arrived on the day he was due, reached all his milestones either when they were expected or before, slept through the night and learned to smile when only a few weeks old. In short, he was a model baby and such a lovely positive in our lives. How lucky we were!

Just after his birth I found a lump in my neck. Actually, I didn't find the lump in my neck, Thomas did. He is very proud of this story now, as a tiny baby I would put him to my shoulder to carry him or pat his back after a feed, he would wave his arms around and occasionally made contact with my neck. It was painful and on checking I realised I had a large lump just below my larynx which appeared when I swallowed. I know I would not have found this if it hadn't had been for baby Thomas. A biopsy showed abnormal cells and I was admitted to Basingstoke Hospital for a total thyroidectomy. Investigations done whilst I was in surgery diagnosed a Papillary Carcinoma (thyroid cancer) which also involved my parathyroid glands. The surgery removed my thyroid gland, two of the four of my parathyroid glands and all the cancer, but my recovery was paused whilst further investigations were made to ensure the cancer had not spread further.

My lovely parents, both now just retired, came to Basingstoke to help whilst I was in hospital so Tony, who works for himself (he has his own Chartered Accountancy practice), could continue to work whilst Mum and Dad looked after Thomas. Part of my thyroid cancer treatment included having a whole-body scan which would reveal any spread of the cancer, which can develop in any gland in the body. Thyroid cells will absorb radioactive iodine so prior to the scan I had to take a radioactive iodine drink and 6 weeks later I would have the scan.

This was all to be done in the Nuclear Medicine department at our nearest specialist unit at Southampton Hospital. It was the most bizarre procedure. I was shown into a room which was empty other than a glass cubicle at the end. I was given a lead container which I was to take into the cubicle with me. My instructions were to unscrew the lid from the lead container and remove a plastic bottle from inside. The glass bottle contained a clear liquid which I then needed drink. I had to remove the lid from this bottle and drink the liquid through a straw, push the straw back into the bottle, reattach the lid and put the whole lot back into the lead container which I left in the cubicle. We were then asked to exit the hospital by the nearest entrance. Other instructions were to go immediately home without stopping anywhere on the way and for 2 weeks I was to avoid pregnant women and children under 1 year old. Tricky when you have a small baby at home.

To ensure the take up of radioactive iodine by any rogue thyroid cells left in my body, I had to be running at a low level of thyroxine, so I must be without thyroxine supplement for the whole of the 6 weeks post thyroidectomy. During this time the levels in my body would gradually reduce which would enable to radioactive iodine take up to be visible on the scan. The effect on me was that my energy levels would decrease and I would experience an increasing weakness in my muscles and clouding of my thoughts. This is exactly what happened, textbook hypothyroidism. I couldn't stand or walk for long, I was tired all the time and I had a dream-like feeling in my head. I gave up driving after an occasion when I was sitting at a junction in my car watching the traffic around me thinking "I'll pull out in a minute". No, I was definitely not safe!

Thomas was 5 months by this time and really starting to move around, he was a lively little boy and needed constant supervision. It was such a challenge for me not to be able to look after him, pick him up or cuddle him. Tony and I returned to Southampton later to have the scan. I was fortunate that my parents were willing to come and stay with us through that time, and that the scan was clear showing that my cancer was removed completely and had not metastasised.

I had mostly recovered but was coming up to the time of returning to work after a year of maternity leave. Parenthood is a life changing event, despite what those career-minded of us might think before their baby is born, it is a time for re-evaluating. For me, being ill at the same time made me change my priorities. Tony was always clear that did not want me to work full time once we had a family, and we were in the fortunate position that we could afford this decision. I wanted to be at home with Thomas during his young years but I loved my job, so I asked whether I could change my contract to work part-time. I was told by my manager that I could not continue as a Head OT on part-time hours, I would need to downgrade. This was not a difficult decision as I knew I wanted to be with Thomas as much as possible, so I took the downgrading, but felt such resentment that I knew I would probably be leaving at the first opportunity!

Two years later I just been offered the perfect new job working for Social Services when I found out I was expecting again. Hastily withdrawing my resignation, I stayed working in Winchester but this time my pregnancy did not go so smoothly.

I had my first antenatal scan in our local hospital at Basingstoke, at 20 weeks, and was asked to come back and see the consultant the following week. I went to the appointment on my own (with 3-year-old Thomas), as we did not foresee any problems. Oh, how naïve we were. The consultant told me that uneven measurements had been detected on my scan, or more precisely, our baby's long bones were not in proportion to the rest of her growth. He told me this was most commonly a feature of Downs Syndrome and he said he would refer us to the Geneticists who were based in Southampton.

It was devastating news, I was completely floored. I didn't know what questions I should be asking or even how to organise my thoughts and I had no idea what should happen next. I really don't remember much about that consultation apart from being asked by a nurse after I came out of the room whether I was okay. I was not okay and drove home in floods of tears with poor little Thomas looking worried. How helpful it would have been if someone had suggested that both Tony & I attend this consultation, which was evidently where we were to be given this life changing news, or to have someone skilled enough to support me, or even be in the appointment with me. I was offered a further meeting with a geneticist to give us more information. Of course, in-between being told our baby had problems, and the appointment with people who hopefully would be able to tell us more, we spent our time imagining all kinds of scenarios and worrying ourselves with what might be.

We saw the Geneticists in Southampton's Princess Anne Hospital (our nearest specialist ante-natal centre) the following week in the hope they would have more information about our baby's uneven growth patterns. We both went to that appointment, we had learned our lesson now, but a further scan didn't show much more than had already been detected. The Geneticist explained the evidence showed the continuing unusual growth of long bones, but no other features consistent with Downs Syndrome had appeared. She suggested that our baby may have Achondroplasia (dwarfism). We were given another appointment in a couple of weeks' time for a further scan. This next consultation was a similar experience in that, apart from short bones, there were no other features typically seen with Achondroplasia so we were booked in for another scan later when our baby would have grown a little more and more obvious features may be seen.

With each scan we had, a new syndrome/diagnosis was suggested and explained to us only to be discounted at the next appointment. The doctors were clearly puzzled, and it was a very stressful and uncertain time. After each new diagnosis I would go home and look up the symptoms, prognosis etc and try to come to terms with the latest bombshell. I know this is not recommended by the professionals involved but of course we wanted to know more. These conditions, apart from Downs Syndrome, Achondroplasia and Campomelia, included Edwards Syndrome which is a condition "incompatible with life" meaning our baby would either not survive birth or would die shortly after being born. Each one of these conditions means lifelong disabilities and learning difficulties. After 5 months of uncertainty, and frankly at times it felt that the doctors were as uncertain about our baby as they were at the first appointment, we made the decision that we would not have any further scans until nearer my term date and that we would love and nurture our baby whatever her future. I was seen again at 34 weeks when this latest scan showed an irregular heartbeat and that growth had slowed completely and I was admitted to Basingstoke Hospital for observation. My maternity leave had started!

I stayed in hospital for almost a week resting and hoping that our baby would hang on for a few more precious days. Mum and Dad came down again to stay with Tony and Thomas and were a great help with childcare, they loved taking Thomas to his playgroup in Winchester and I was glad to see them visiting me in hospital. The thing that kept me occupied mainly during that week was that I was making sugar flowers for a friend's wedding cake so I took it all into the maternity ward with me and my production line of little roses, carnations and blossoms definitely benefited from my confinement and endless hours to kill. You will be glad to know that the sugar flowers were finished in time for the wedding and I handed them over in the most strange of circumstances when my bride-to-be friend came to the hospital to collect them. I was monitored constantly during this week until one morning our baby's heartbeat became very irregular, she was in distress. I was to have a caesarean section as it appeared her heart was not strong enough to survive the normal labour and birth process and we were warned that it was very likely that she would not survive at all, that she would be still-born, or incompatible with life. I phoned Tony at work and it was arranged for later that morning.

I was prepared for the Caesarean section and Tony was gloved and gowned ready to join me in theatres. Our Paediatrician arrived just as Tony was coming into the theatre and commented to him "better news about the latest scan from Southampton". If there was ever an example of how important it is to read the patient's notes before commenting this was it. We were trying to prepare ourselves for losing our baby, the whole reason we were all there was because she was in distress. He was clearly not up to speed on the events since my admission to Basingstoke.

Catherine was born on 2nd September 1999, five weeks early weighing 1.29 kg (2 lbs 13oz), breathing independently after a little help and was whisked away to an incubator in Neonatal Intensive Care.

Despite the uncertainty of my pregnancy, we were totally unprepared for having a tiny baby in an incubator. We suddenly found ourselves in a world out of our control, everything we knew about being parents changed. Catherine was beautiful but oh so tiny. We all just gazed at her through the incubator wondering at how small and unfinished she appeared, her skin looked translucent.

I had never been in a Neonatal Intensive Care Unit before (NICU) and the whole experience was like entering another world. The first thing that hits you is the heat which was heightened by the fact that it was early September, and we were experiencing an Indian summer. Once in the Unit there are constant alarms bleeping and bonging, rows of machines and monitors all doing the vital work of keeping tiny babies alive, busy staff, tired and emotional parents and a line of incubators containing tiny scraps of life. Catherine's incubator was next to two twin girls, one of whom had Edward's syndrome, and it was known that she would not be expected to live. I had become friendly with her Mum who was in the next room to me on the ante-natal ward in my last few days of pregnancy. Her twins were already born, and she had introduced me to the two little girls. I was really upset when this brave Mum told me her poorly baby had died – it was just too close to home.

We have kept in touch though, and I know her surviving twin (who did not have any underlying health issues aside from being premature) is doing well and is now studying to be a Paediatric nurse. Such bonds are formed with parents who are going through similar experiences and although this was an intensely emotional time we found we shared a similar sense of humour and this most certainly kept us sane. We found it so funny to be in the "milking room" which was definitely one of the most strange aspects of neonates, where we sat looking like very un-gorgeous non-yummy mummies attached to machines helping us express milk, naming ourselves Daisy and Buttercup (well it seemed funny at the time)! We could then feed the milk to our babies whilst still in their incubators, through a NG (naso gastric) tube which passed through their noses directly into their stomachs, until such time as they would form their sucking reflex.

We held Catherine for the first time when she was only a few hours hold. I sat in a comfy armchair next to her incubator and the nurse lifted her out, wrapped her in a blanket, being careful of leads and tubes, and handed her to me. She weighed so little it felt as though I was lifting an empty blanket and we just stared in wonder at this tiny bundle of skin and bone. Tony, Thomas and I took it in turns to hold her but she seemed so fragile as we cuddled her, only for short periods, so she did not get cold. We were introduced to the concept of "kangaroo care" when she was a few days old. This is the most moving experience where your tiny baby is tucked inside your shirt to cuddle skin against skin. It was beautiful, and really felt like a miracle. We were taught how to give her feeds via the nasogastric tube and even things we knew how to do, like nappy changes, needed relearning and a new confidence to do them through the incubator port holes.

Having had a caesarean meant I stayed on the post-natal ward for a few days, Tony would bring Thomas into neonates each morning so they could spend time with me and Catherine.

At two days old and still in her incubator Catherine became critically unwell, all her vital signs were haywire, she suffered seizures and could not breathe for herself. She had developed septicaemia (sepsis). We were not able to be with her while the doctors were working with her and she was subsequently sedated and intubated (this is where a breathing tube is inserted through the mouth into the lungs and attached to respirator to do the work of breathing for her). We were told that she would remain on the ventilator and reviewed in the morning.

She had been doing so well since birth and this illness seemed to come from nowhere. The experience was frightening, impossible to describe how numb you can feel when emotions, already in such a heightened state from the birth, are thrown further into chaos. Once Catherine appeared to be in a more stable state with the ventilator breathing for her, the nurses on my ward suggested I had a sedative myself, and I blocked out a few hours that night. When I went down to the Neonatal Unit the next morning Catherine was still intubated and unconscious, there was nothing to do but sit and watch. The nurses coming on shift were all surprisingly positive that she was still holding her own, with my knowledge of health care professionals I knew that the looks on their faces spoke more. They had not expected her to still be with us.

She was slowly weaned off the ventilator after 2 days as she was breathing for herself again, her feeding gradually began to improve and thankfully there were no further blips. Our Paediatrician explained the damage that this episode would have caused to Catherine and warned us to expect the worst - that although she was better at the moment, anything could change over the next few days, and if she should survive, would probably have brain damage causing problems with mobility, vision and hearing.

Although it took some years for the true effect of that episode to become evident, that day, ours and Thomas's lives changed forever. As well as parents and sibling we were to become carers.

Despite being tiny, Catherine was made of strong stuff and always went by her very own rule book!

She continued to recover and began to grow and after three weeks was moved out of her incubator into a hot cot, which felt like a huge positive milestone. Now she had put on weight she looked more like the sort of baby we were used to! We could pick her up whenever we wanted and when she began to drink my expressed milk from a bottle her NG tube could be removed. Her discharge home was planned for when she reached her target weight of 4lbs.

We had visitors all the way through our neonates' experience, but I particularly remember those that came just after Catherine was born. It was hard to be positive when we were being prepared for the worst, and one of our visitors from that time has told me she was very affected by the intensity of the situation, the heat and just how small and vulnerable Catherine was. I loved visitors, they really distracted from the worry, and brought news of the outside world. It was such a hot summer and being in neonates felt like being in an incubator ourselves. Some of my OT friends from Winchester came to visit once Catherine was stable and starting to grow, we went outside to sit on the scorched grass with cold drinks, it was lovely to have some fresh air and they brought their usual laughter and sense of the ridiculous with them, it was just the tonic!

I was discharged home from hospital following my caesarean at 5 days, without Catherine, as I was ready for discharge long before she was. Tony picked me up and we left the Unit alone. There were no cheery goodbyes from the staff as there had been 3 years earlier when I left the hospital after giving birth to baby Thomas, it was very emotional. I felt bereft without our baby as I walked in through our front door at home remembering that I had left 10 days before to attend a routine appointment, but so much had happened during that time it felt like a lifetime ago.

I was still recovering from the caesarean and so was not able to drive for up to 6 weeks, so even visiting Catherine meant relying on others to take me. I struggled with the baby blues and found the separation of being at home whilst she was still in intensive care really hard, and we were very worried about her future. I did spend as much time as possible with her and I was really lucky that Thomas was fairly content to play in the room. He loved books, which was good for Catherine too and I would read to them both. I just wanted to hold and feed her, and like countless others before me who have had to leave babies in the Neonatal Unit, and those whose babies have not survived, I ached for her physically too. I remember one morning having walked to our local shops with Thomas and hearing a baby cry, I experienced the let-down reflex of my milk and just felt overwhelmed with emotion.

We were able to take our much-loved little girl home after 5 weeks in Neonates, by now she had put on a whole pound in weight! (she weighed 3 lbs, 12 oz) and learned to adapt our family life around her frequent slow feeds and unpredictable short sleeps. So as not to disrupt his life more than necessary, Thomas continued to attend his childminder and playgroup in Winchester. He was a content and happy boy who loved sitting with me and Catherine (and his books) while she took an hour to drink an ounce of milk.

We settled into a routine of sorts. We were all very proud of our tiny baby and we treated her as we had done with our Thomas, going out and about as much as possible. Premature baby clothes and equipment were not so easy to find then, so we improvised, I made a small padded cushion for her to sit on so she was safer in her standard car seat, and Mum bought a dolls clothes pattern and knitted lots of little socks and cardigans in different colours for her. Thomas embraced his role as her big brother and would protect her and keep an eye on her wherever we were. He would check on her regularly to make sure she was ok, to move her position if she was laying, or to wheel her away with him if she was in her buggy. He would tell me if he thought she needed something and I would often find him sitting next to her if she was in her car seat on the floor or lying next to her under her baby gym.

3

POORLY

When we left neonates we were told that we would have "open access" to the children's assessment ward at Basingstoke Hospital also known as Charlie's Day Unit which meant we could take Catherine directly to hospital when she was unwell, rather than having to waste precious time going to our GP for referral. Little did we know how helpful this would be. We were racing through Autumn and Winter was on its way. We had no idea what this meant in terms of our vulnerable baby, but the Winter infection bugs arrived as usual, this time with serious effect. As we neared Christmas, Catherine by now aged 3 ½ months, had a cold and battled all through

Christmas Day but by Boxing Day we realised she was struggling to breathe.

We took Thomas across the road to our neighbours, who were always wonderfully supportive and spoilt him rotten, and we took Catherine to Basingstoke hospital (the first of so many visits during her first year, I gave up counting after 20) where she was rushed to their High Dependency Unit. Her oxygen levels were in her boots and her work of breathing meant her respiratory rate was over 80 per minute (should be below 40). She continued to struggle and we were told that she would need to be ventilated and transferred to Southampton General Hospital, our nearest children's intensive care unit (a 2 hour round trip from our home in Basingstoke), if she did not improve soon.

This was our first experience of how quickly she could become seriously unwell. We were horrified that she could be back on a ventilator and in intensive care, but also that she would have to be transferred to another city for her care.

Catherine had been in the Basingstoke High Dependency Unit for 24 hours now and she continued to struggle. We were told that she must be ventilated and transferred to a Paediatric Intensive Care Unit (PICU) which indeed meant that she would be taken by blue light ambulance to

Southampton. We were taken out of her room and to a waiting room where we stood wordlessly and helplessly whilst she was intubated by our own Paediatrician. We then waited for the Retrieval Team. This a specialist team of doctors and paramedics who arrived in a specialist ambulance which carries all the kit required to transport a ventilated baby in an incubator. She was prepared to transfer onto a stretcher with portable ventilation equipment, portable monitors and oxygen and handed over completely to the retrieval team, who took her by emergency ambulance to Southampton.

We were not allowed to travel with Catherine in the ambulance and were told to wait a while before driving down to see her so that we were not following them. We collected Thomas from where he had been playing with friends and set off. We arrived at the General about half an hour after her, and made our way up to PICU. We were shown into a waiting room, where we were told that we could not see her yet as the journey had upset her and the doctors were working with her. We waited an endless wait and were finally taken to see her. That first sight was one to take my breath away. Contrast to the unit in Basingstoke NICU, Southampton General PICU is many times the size with more and larger equipment, full sized beds and with a nurse assigned to each child. Seeing Catherine in a full sized hospital bed, looking so small (although she was 3 months old she still only weighed 5lbs) with her face obscured by a mask and tubes, and surrounded by banks of machines keeping her alive, was heart breaking.

The intense and varied range of emotions we went through during that admission is so difficult to describe, fear and helplessness mainly, but love and pride too. At the time of this first PICU admission parents were not allowed to stay with children in Southampton Intensive Care Unit, and there was no accommodation available in the hospital. I was offered a room in a house across the hospital grounds for relatives of children and adults in Intensive and Coronary Care Units. Tony went home to look after Thomas. I shared my room with a lady whose husband was in the Coronary Care Unit after suffering a heart attack on Christmas Day. It felt such a surreal experience to be living in this scary world of intense emotions and sharing my trauma and tears with strangers.

Later, accommodation for parents was built across the corridor from PICU, making staying over a little easier, although it was always hard to have the family divided. Now they have Ronald Macdonald house which is apparently amazing although I have never seen it myself. It is understood how very difficult it is for families to be away from their children, plus paediatrics has changed in its approach to not only encourage parents to care for their children, it is expected. My parents came down again to help, and particularly to look after Thomas, to allow Tony to be with me and Catherine (and try to work – this was his busiest time of year), and again, it would have been so hard for us to manage without their willingness to help.

During this admission we celebrated New Year. It was year 2000, everyone remembers where they were for the Millennium and we are absolutely no exception. Every New Year Tony and I are reminded that we spent that last midnight of 1999 together in Southampton Hospital with Catherine so poorly. We watched out of the window near her hospital bed in Intensive Care, as the fireworks showered over the City, people were celebrating, and we shared a glass of alcohol-free bubbly with the nurses. We then walked across the car park with the sound of fireworks echoing across the city, to my shared room. Tony left me and drove home to join my Mum and Dad, who we had left a bottle of real Champagne for, and a sleeping Thomas. Oh yes, we will always remember where we were for the Millennium.

Catherine very slowly recovered from her bronchiolitis, was weaned off the ventilator, and once breathing independently, was transferred to a medical ward. Before discharge home from hospital, we attended an appointment with a

Consultant Neurologist. She informed us that Catherine was showing signs of brain damage and neuro abnormalities, this was what we had been warned about following her intubation at 2 days old, the prognosis given us then was starting to become evident. She was discharged home once oxygen levels and feeds were on the up but was not back to health for some while after that. She came home with an NG tube for feeding again and was constantly wheezy and coughing, she was obviously still feeling unwell for weeks. Looking after Catherine at home with NG tube in place was new to us and poor Catherine looked so forlorn, she was struggling to feed and although we hated that she needed it, it did mean we could get some calories into her. It felt an enormous responsibility to be caring for and nurturing our still tiny baby who was now reliant on equipment and medication, she was very unsettled much of the time. Over time she slowly improved, the NG was removed and she regained the weight she had lost whilst so poorly.

Although she eventually got over this episode, it was not long before we were back in Basingstoke hospital with another chest infection, a pattern that was repeated many times over the next 2 years. She was experiencing reflux (common with small babies where their stomachs are not able to keep milk down) and this was starting to cause her pain as well as recurrent chest infections. We were allocated a Children's Community Nurse (CCN) who was based in Basingstoke Hospital and was our link between hospital and home, although it seemed that we spent more time in hospital than at home for the first 2 years of Catherine's life. We were lucky that we had the same Community Nurse for the whole of Catherine's life, so she came to know everything about Catherine and her problems, and apart from being way too busy she was skilled, efficient and reassuring.

Before our confident CCN came into our lives, we were supported in the usual way by a Health Visitor and had been attending baby clinics at our local surgery. The Health Visitors who had been so helpful and encouraging when Thomas was a baby seemed out of their depth with all my questions about premature baby care. When we should start weaning, what to do about the reflux, and how to protect her from the normal bugs which seemed to be so serious for Catherine. The baby clinic was so unsupportive I stopped going, they just seemed focussed on Catherine's growth percentiles and weight gain. I felt responsible for the lack of development, it was distressing to see how she "failed to thrive" as it was described, and it was woeful watching them plot her progress chart. It was months before she made it onto the Percentile chart and even then, she was a long way from where she should be. I did go back to the Neonatal Unit at one point to see whether they had any of the information I was looking for, or contact for a local support group for Mums of premature babies but there was nothing at that time.

I wonder how we would have managed without the incredible support we had from neighbours and friends through those early years. We were absolutely blessed to have the most caring neighbours living across the road. I would take Thomas over there for a drink each afternoon throughout my difficult pregnancy, and Catherine's early years. These neighbours had their own growing family of boisterous boys and there were often other neighbours there too, it was an enjoyable thing to look forward to each day. If it was too much, they never said, and always seemed happy to see us. After Catherine was born, they were such a support, especially when she was poorly, when everything seemed so gloomy, they were positive and cheerful. They would offer to look after Thomas if we needed to take Catherine to hospital urgently, and he loved being spoilt by them. They will never know how reassuring it was to have them just across the road.

Tony has always regularly attended his local church and is a member of the Catenian Association, a wonderful group of people who meet regularly and have always been very supportive to our family. Tony took both children to church each week, they were part of the Catholic community and were embraced by the congregation and priest in their empathic way, and were always so positive. Catherine loved everything about going to church. Her disabilities meant that she was not able to interact unless people interacted with her, but being in church meant she was able to experience music, singing and speaking voices, and human contact with the sign of peace (where people would hold her hand) and the priest's blessing (a hand rested on her head) and everyone made a fuss of her. It also gave me an hour of peace and quiet at home on a Sunday morning!

Those first two years were a very difficult time for all of us, Catherine was a little girl who was poorly and in pain. Bottle feeding had become even more challenging and could take several hours a day (and invariably was sicked back up again), or after a hospital admission was again via an NG tube. Although the tube helped in some ways, it was a curse in others, as Catherine would vomit it out of her mouth which then involved me having to take both children up to the hospital to have it replaced. We were there so often I felt this was an unnecessary use of their resources when I could learn to replace it myself. Our Community Children's Nurse showed me how to do the procedure and this saved some pressure on our stressed-out family.

Our Paediatrician confirmed that Catherine's breathing problems were caused by oesophageal reflux, where her stomach contents and acid flowed back up into her throat and lungs causing constant pain and infection. We permanently carried a cloth "sick rag" everywhere with us, woe betide the person who held Catherine without this important piece of kit. One morning Tony was ready to leave the house wearing a newly dry-cleaned suit and foolishly decided to have a quick cuddle with Catherine before leaving. She chose that moment to sick up her whole feed onto his legs, she was lethal and that was the end of the clean suit!

We now used our "open access" card regularly as Catherine would often become very unwell very quickly and it meant that she had the treatment she needed without delay, normally oxygen, nebulisers and antibiotics. Once she recovered, which she always did but probably slowly added to her disabilities, we were discharged home and back into the care of our CCN and GP.

I came to know our GP well during Catherine's first years, we seemed to be at the surgery most weeks for appointments or prescriptions. She was another positive for me, she was so supportive, where possible would give advice over the phone to save us having to visit. After a hospital admission we would often be discharged with only a couple of days' worth of medication. This added unnecessary stress that as well as looking after our just-discharged still poorly child we needed to go out to the surgery to get more medication. Our GP would arrange a repeat prescription and send it directly to the pharmacy without making us attend the surgery. We were extremely lucky to have the same GP throughout Catherine's life. She got used to my attempts at trying to avoid a hospital admission, hoping she could prescribe something miraculous, these emergency appointments mostly ended with her saying "I'm really sorry but you need to take her in". Ah well, it was worth a try!

4

EARLY YEARS

Despite all her struggles, Catherine smiled for the first time at 11 months old. What a wonderful thing - we were delighted – she had been close to doing this for a while and with lots of cooing and encouragement, we had our first little smile. And from then on, when she was well, she smiled and smiled! In fact, sometimes even when she wasn't well, sometimes even when she was in hospital, and despite how bad she must have felt, she would still smile. She had a lovely first birthday with lots of new clothes age 3-6 months for her to grow into. She still only weighed 10 lbs.

Life for me and Catherine became an endless round of appointments. I found this aspect particularly difficult. I have read lots of articles about how isolating it is to be a carer and I can totally vouch for that. We had our house invaded by therapists, nurses and portage workers. I use the word "invaded" because although they were sensitive enough, I still felt I had to tidy up, make them coffee and try to make myself available to help their sessions with Catherine, and of course, Thomas was too young to understand why they didn't want to play with him too.

The hospital appointments meant Thomas coming with us, and I know I was blessed that he was such a content boy, but I was very aware that he was missing out. Often there were times that activities and days out with friends had to be cancelled as Catherine was ill. Being the happy positive child that he was, and because of his unique bond with Catherine, he accepted this and when I apologised to him, sometimes I could not hide my exasperation at events, he would say "it's not Catherine's fault"! What a lovely nature he has, he always took huge interest in all her cares and therapies, he would keep an eye her sats monitor and oxygen levels when she was in hospital. When he was brought in for a visit he would run into her cubicle on the Children's ward and climb into her cot to give her a cuddle. Not surprisingly, she responded to him more than anyone else.

We had become one of Basingstoke Hospital's regular families, and my main social life revolved around being friends with other parents of children on the ward and the staff who worked there. It was depressing seeing other children come in poorly, whose parents were all consumed with their anxieties, their usually well child suddenly stricken with an unexpected emergency. Some would have surgery, but most of these children within a few days would begin to recover and go home. So many came and went, whilst Catherine was still poorly, her long term needs gradually becoming evident. But this was the first time I was able to meet and share experiences with the mothers of other special needs children which was where I found some of my most valuable support over the rest of her life. We numbered a few regulars whose children had long term or chronic health conditions and would meet in the parent's kitchen at all hours of day or night, or in the playroom with our other siblings, we shared stories and support of each other. We also took each other's stories to heart, the connection between special needs parents is extraordinary and similar emotions are shared.

It was around this time that I was due to return to work after my year's maternity leave. I was torn about what to do but went back to my job in Winchester Hospital on the same part time hours as before. Goodness what a challenge it was to have both children ready with all appropriate equipment and medications, to get to the childminder, who lived between Basingstoke and Winchester, and me to work by 8.30 am. Often Catherine would have vomited up her morning meds and I would need her to have another feed. Our childminder was extraordinary, she coped with most of what was being asked of her, Catherine's long and difficult bottle feeds, frequent vomiting and all manner of medication to be given. Thomas was happy there, she used to walk him to a little playgroup with her other young charges all of whom he loved. It was the perfect place for him, he was loved and nurtured there, I had a good relationship with her, which meant I could concentrate on work when she cared for the children.

However, as Catherine's health continued to be unpredictable, I worried that we were far away from the hospital and if she became unwell, I would need to collect her which would also would mean taking Thomas out of nursery so we could go back to Basingstoke. I made the decision to give up work after four months, it was just too exhausting to be awake all night with Catherine and try to function the next day in a busy role at work.

However, I lasted only a few weeks as an "at home" Mum, I realised that being exhausted did not feel any better because I was not at work and I was happier being busy however bad I felt. I had found it very stressful to have my days and nights totally focussed on caring and home making. I became far too worried about having a tidy home and obsessing about things I had no control over, like the right kind of support being available for children with disabilities without everything being a fight. Of course, these things will always bother me but they can be someone else's battle! It was clear that I need to work for my sanity, and to have a routine to my week, I needed a purpose in my life other than being at home worrying about Catherine's care. I was lucky to have found such a rewarding career and so far had always worked with lovely supportive teams. So during this time of regular hospital admissions for Catherine, I moved from working in Winchester to Basingstoke, much nearer home.

I started working two days a week for the Basingstoke Wheelchair Service which at that time consisted of a very small team of two therapists and admin support. Both of us OTs divided the referrals for adults and children's wheelchairs and seating between us. I really enjoyed the variety of clinics and home visits. I was building on my understanding of the importance of posture in managing pain and fatigue, which would be so helpful in our family life later on.

By her second year it seemed that Catherine was almost permanently in hospital with her head in a clear plastic oxygen box. We knew that her breathing problems stemmed from her reflux which we were told could be treated by having an operation (fundoplication) to build a "valve" at the top of her stomach to prevent her being sick and stop stomach contents going into her lungs. She would also have a gastrostomy which would provide a feeding tube directly into her stomach to give her the nutrition she was being denied by her sickness.

We were referred back to Southampton and met the surgeon who explained what was involved in the operation. We were horrified at the description of what would happen and the size of the scar Catherine would be left with, but it seemed there was no alternative. I am convinced she would not have survived another winter of chest infections. It also helped that we felt we could trust the surgeon, he was a great communicator (unlike so many others!) and really took the trouble to explain, and make sure we knew exactly what we were consenting to.

To cope with such a major operation, she needed to be strong enough and weigh enough to have the resources to recover. This was the biggest hurdle. Catherine needed to gain weight but her constant sickness, chest infections and pain meant that any good patch of being well and thriving was always followed by a hospital admission when she was not able to tolerate feed and would lose precious ounces. She was waking 8 or 9 times a night and cried endlessly. She had days when she was so sick she would have seizures. We were exhausted and felt helpless, as she was clearly in pain, not thriving and not developing.

Catherine was now attending the nearest nursery to my work, which was a mainstream nursery but based in Basingstoke hospital grounds, so it suited us all better, being local and near my work. However, an ordinary nursery looking after a poorly baby with a feeding tube is not a good mix. The other children used to pull the tube out or Catherine would vomit it out of her mouth. Their nursery nurses were really caring but were not staffed well enough for Catherine to always have a one-to-one and I was regularly called to give advice or to come and replace her tube. One day I was at work, on a home visit to a do a wheelchair assessment for a patient who was right on the edge of our geographical area. I had just pulled up outside the house when the office rang me to say Catherine's nursery had called, she was very unwell, struggling to breathe. I phoned them immediately and had to explain that even if I turned round and came back now it would take me an hour and it sounded as though Catherine needed immediate help, they should call an ambulance. When I got back to Basingstoke she had been admitted to the High Dependency Unit and was back on oxygen again.

This was one of the factors which helped me decide on another career move. I had been working for the Wheelchair Service now for a year or so, and I loved the job, but the work involved community visiting. I would run assessment clinics in Basingstoke which was local to home, but community visits could take me all over the far corners of our rural area of North Hampshire. It was this that worried me. I couldn't be available when Catherine needed me if I was away from Basingstoke. I felt the responsibility of being only one of two therapists covering all patients referred for wheelchair assessments. I hated having to cancel appointments, but this was unavoidable when Catherine was unwell and needed to be at home.

I applied and was accepted for a job in Basingstoke hospital working in Elective Orthopaedics. The team consisted of Occupational Therapists and Physiotherapists and the nature of the work meant that we planned the day's work each morning, dividing between us the patients who needed to be seen. We prepared patients for joint replacement surgery, with advice and equipment provided during a pre-op assessment clinic and post-surgery our patients would receive rehab on the orthopaedic ward and attend follow up clinics after discharge.

It was a very positive area in which to work, we would see our patients before surgery when their pain and reduced movements were affecting their daily lives, and then 6 weeks later most would return for a post-op clinic with their raised toilet seat in a bag, crutches under their arms and smiles on their faces. The speed and turnover of patients in this area of orthopaedics meant we did not carry our own caseloads but worked in a very flexible way, which really suited my life at that time, and I was based near home.

I still feel anxious when I remember Catherine's second winter. She was on medication for her digestion, acid reflux, seizures, and high muscle tone, special high calorie milk with added vitamins and thickener, and endless Calpol and Neurofen, but none of it seemed to help and she cried and cried. We really felt desperate trying to care for our very stressed out baby and the only time she seemed to calm was when she was sucking on her dummy or bottle of milk. Although she did not really want the milk, as the level didn't go down, I think the only time she did not suffer from reflux was when she was swallowing which accounted for what we used to call her "dummy dependency".

One of the difficulties especially in those early days, but really all through Catherine's life, was knowing when we had reached the limit of what we could do for her and when to call for help. We didn't know when she needed oxygen or antibiotics as she seemed to be wheezy and struggling to breathe much of the time, even when just discharged from hospital. She had a permanent cough which seemed to send her whole body into spasm and her face would turn puce. When we were out, and Catherine had a coughing fit, people would turn round with disapproving looks and then be astonished to see a little girl in a buggy rather than an old drunk leaning against a lamppost! But joking aside, we often felt the weight of responsibility of looking after our poorly little girl and trying to assess when she needed medical intervention, balanced against trying not to overreact and take her unnecessarily to hospital.

The August before her 2nd birthday in September 2001 Catherine finally reached her target weight to have the fundoplication, to prevent her reflux and hopefully reduce chest infections, and the gastrostomy to enable feeding through a tube directly into her stomach. We knew she needed this vital surgery before the next winter's bugs arrived. This was her first major surgery and again we would be back in Southampton General, and again the family would be divided while I stayed with her, and Tony was taking Thomas to and from school, with the help of my regular visitor parents.

The lead up to the surgery was a tense time for us as Catherine was in Basingstoke Hospital recovering from another chest infection until the day of the operation. We knew that the surgery would be delayed if it was felt she was not well enough to cope. By the day of the surgery it was decided she would go to Southampton and be assessed. We were grateful for the experience of our friendly Paediatric Surgeon who was to perform the operation, he wasn't fazed at all by her very recent illness and pointed out that this was the whole reason she needed the surgery. Although he had been very patient in explaining exactly what was involved (with some interesting looking diagrams) but he had also voiced concern that the size of Catherine's stomach may make the surgery difficult; she had a condition called microgastria (small stomach).

After lots of organising of care of Thomas and packing mountains of equipment and meds for Catherine, we were admitted to Southampton General for her operation. Once on the ward I was given the smallest hospital gown I had ever seen to dress her in (with teddy bears printed on it – somehow these made the whole thing seem even more heart rending) and we went down to theatres with Catherine in her buggy. I was told she would be in theatre for an hour or so. I later learned to take these predictions with a pinch of salt as, of course, Catherine never followed their rule book. But this was her first operation and after kissing her goodbye at the anaesthetic room, I took her empty buggy back to the ward and then set off to find a strong coffee and watch the clock. The anaesthetist was a very business-like and experienced female doctor who gave me huge confidence, but I probably don't need to tell you how hard that that kiss goodbye was; leaving your baby in the hands of a surgical team is one of the hardest things for a parent to do, and my mind was filled with dread as I walked back to the ward with her buggy.

I drank my coffee in record time, paced the floor and slowly the hour ticked on, I returned to the surgical ward as instructed but there was no news yet so I sat by her empty bed and waited. I started checking for any news at the nurses' station after an hour, 1 ½ and two hours, with no news. After 2 ½ hours I was getting increasingly distressed, one of the nurses took pity on me and called down to theatres again. This time I was told Catherine was out of surgery but not ready to come back to the ward. It was after 4 hours, by which time I was frantic, that they said she was in resus but she was not coping well. Eventually I was told I could go down to see her, and I ran. I couldn't wait for a lift, I just ran down the 4 floors to theatres! When I got to the door of the resus ward, I could hear her cries, I was met by one of the nurses who said she was "unsettled". This word covers a huge range of different meanings in medical-speak and Catherine was in a desperate state. She was screaming into her oxygen mask, retching, coughing, and thrusting around on the bed with an enormous bandage covering her chest and abdomen. I crossed the room in record time to pick her up (not easy, it took me and 2 nurses to pick up our writhing little girl and avoid getting tangled in the mass of monitors, drains and oxygen tubing) and cuddled her. Oh my goodness how we both needed that cuddle! She calmed down after a while, although still needing high amounts of oxygen, and we were eventually able to leave theatres lying on her bed with her still in my arms, to the Paediatric High Dependency Unit.

The anaesthetist visited us once she had finished her patient list and spent some time with us, as did the surgeon who was happy with how the operation had gone and felt the effects would be very beneficial to Catherine. These doctors were so understanding and empathetic, in fact, when we returned a few months later for Catherine to have further surgery (an abdominal hernia repair), the same anaesthetist that time allowed me to come into theatres to be with her right until the point of intubation, and after the op I was called much earlier into resus to hold Catherine and try and prevent the distress she had experienced that first time.

We stayed in HDU needing breathing support for several days, with Catherine making slow progress. We were in a bed space next to a little boy who was 6 months older than Catherine, who had come speeding onto the ward, full of beans, whizzing along using a tiny walking frame causing everyone to fall instantly in love with him as he went! He had the same operation as Catherine and also had a gastrostomy tube in his stomach now. He too ended up coming to HDU following the op and like Catherine, had scary dips in his oxygen levels and other machine-bleeping problems. His mum and I instantly connected (he had a chromosomal abnormality so would also have long term disabilities) and it is reassuring how such a friendship can make the worst situation more bearable. She told me that her little son also had a history of not following a predictable path, just like Catherine. She was right! As soon as one of their machines stopped alarming, the other would start. They kept the nurses busy that admission!

We stayed friends for years and met again on the medical wards occasionally, it was always an easier admission when they were there with us. I know the reason we were there was because our children were poorly but it always felt like something of a reunion, it was better for Catherine when her little friend was on the ward with us, he was so lively, and it was definitely better for me. We would order take-aways to be delivered to the hospital and used to have feeding pump races, the first to set up their child's feeding pump was the winner, a bit like Top Gear for special needs mums! It was quality company that was rare to find.

Eventually we were transferred back to the general surgical ward and I was shown how to care for the newly formed gastrostomy and the huge dressing which covered the line of stitches down Catherine's abdomen. It was 2 weeks from surgery until she was well enough to leave hospital and I was confident with her care.

Tony and Thomas came to visit us each day, which was such a lovely thing to look forward to. The days are long in hospital and again we saw other children come in for their operations, get well and go home whilst we were still there, apart from our new friends who it seemed were in exactly the same unpredictable boat as us. I remember on one Sunday afternoon, I heard Thomas's voice long before I saw him as he raced up the ward holding a finger in the air shouting that he had been stung on it by a wasp. I loved this reminder of the normality of the world outside the hospital where a child with a wasp sting is more demanding of attention than the silent child lying in the hospital bed attached to machines, and how he cheered the whole ward up with his dramatic story.

We were discharged home with mountains of equipment, feeding pump, bottles to attach to the feeding pump, extension tubes and giving sets for the feed, syringes for winding and medication and take-home medicines. I had been taught how to give bolus feeds (where a large syringe is used with a tube to give a feed through the gastrostomy) and set up and operate her feeding pump, to give formula via her gastrostomy button, and medication through port in the giving set, how to release her wind and care for the skin. It was such a responsibility and I now needed to teach Tony how to do all these cares too. I know I am so lucky that Tony was prepared to learn and take turns with Catherine's care which became increasingly equipment dependent. He too learned to do all of it and was more than happy to share and take over when he needed to. We used our own medication chart to keep her safe, that way we could see what was needed and when, and whether it had already been done by the other one of us, and when.

Following this operation, the wound down the middle of Catherine's abdomen became infected. It felt as though each problem solved would cause another new difficulty to overcome. Our Community Children's Nurse was a regular visitor again and gradually with her support we became adept at dealing with all the equipment, ordering supplies and judging when to progress her care plan. The fundoplication made a huge difference to her general health as she had stopped being sick. At various times during her life I used to keep a diary and an entry made just after her fundoplication read that she had been out of hospital for 8 weeks which was a record.

5

DIAGNOSIS

Following her surgery Catherine was having periods of being well and we had great hopes for her development. I know that I had difficulty accepting what we had been told about her future. Whilst her health had been so ill, I felt it was unfair to judge her development when she was struggling to just breathe, feed and grow. During periods of being well however, she was still not learning how to make intentional movements, follow or track with her eyes or show any signs of moving herself around. Before her surgery we had asked to know more about a diagnosis or a reason for the lack of development. We had been told that it was unsafe to have a diagnostic MRI scan until she was well enough to have the anaesthetic required to undertake the scan. This was the only concrete way of knowing the extent of her brain damage, which even I had to admit was becoming apparent.

After her stomach surgery, Catherine's sickness reduced, and it was decided she would be able to cope with the anaesthetic required for her brain scan. I don't think our Paediatrician really understood why we wanted to know more about the cause of Catherine's lack of development but it was so hard to know how best to help her and what we could expect from her future. To be told that her future will "not be rosy" and she will have a lifetime of dependency on equipment is hard to accept without understanding the reason. The scan would hopefully shed light on the causes of her lack of development.

Back to Southampton Hospital, back to the same anaesthetist (a lady who I was coming to know well!) but this time for a routine procedure. Again, I went for a walk whilst our 3 year old Catherine was prepared to pass through the enormous noisy MRI scanner. Heaven only knows how frightening the whole thing must have been for her, although she was not awake for the actual scan, but at least it was over within an hour and we were back on the Day Unit within two hours (again after oxygen), and home that evening. We were given an appointment to see the Neurologist a few weeks later. The results were catastrophic. He showed us the scan image and explained that she had widespread brain damage, cysts, and what appeared to be holes in all areas of her brain. The Neurologist, who must have been absent when bedside manner was being taught at medical school, described it as a "shot gun effect", a dreadful description for what was appalling news for us and we were told her prognosis was poor. Although this evidence did not explain the cause of her brain damage, it explained why Catherine's development was not progressing and he told us she would not walk or talk and would have profound learning difficulties.

I understand that it is important that doctors explain the facts and the likely effect of their findings on the life of the child in their care, but I am sad that none of the consultants we were under during those early years encouraged us to see any positives or explain that children with profound and multiple difficulties can have a good quality of life. Most of our friends who have children with extra needs have an endless repertoire of extraordinary and heart-warming stories to tell which demonstrate the wonderful personalities of their children.

The neurologist's prognosis proved to be accurate, Catherine never did walk or talk, or gain any purposeful movement, and she did have profound learning difficulties. But she also had marvellous strength of character, sense of humour and love for family and friends. She had a love of life and over the years so many people told me that she had had a lasting and emotional effect on them, in fact, it was overwhelming to see how everyone who met her quickly fell in love with her.

Over the next few years, emergency admissions thankfully reduced although never stopped, and I always had a bag packed with basic supplies of feed & tubes, syringes, nappies and clothes ready for an unexpected hospital admission all through her life.

After her MRI, which had been so shocking, we did at least feel we knew more about how life would be. We knew Catherine's disabilities would be profound and lifelong. We would always be her advocates but we now also had a label of sorts which helps in this world where funding and resources are limited and have to be fought over.

We were referred to a special needs playscheme at one of our local Special Schools. I would stay with Catherine when we went here and found so much support, again from parents (actually all Mums) who attended this group. I remember having an amazing conversation with another Mum about clearing up refluxed vomit – her son also used to vomit 8 to 9 times a day and we exchanged graphic stories about how far projectile vomit can travel from the mouth of a small child. Where else would I have been comfortable talking about such things?!

I loved this play group and hoped Catherine would go to school here. This was a school for children with primarily physical difficulties. Tony and I attended a review around the time we would be thinking of applying, during this meeting we were told that her learning difficulty was too profound and could not be best met here. They told us we should be applying to Limington House School (where she did go and was very happy), because they were more equipped to cope with all her disabilities. They were very sensitive about giving us this information, but this was a huge blow and another indication that Catherine was not developing as we hoped.

We went to look round Limington House School, a Special School for children with severe to profound learning difficulties. As parents of a small child it was very shocking to see the older children in wheelchairs with seating systems giving them maximum support, needing help with all their personal care, and hoisted for transfers. I really was not able to cope with this glimpse into the future and convinced myself that this would not be how Catherine would grow. At that stage I was not ready to think that far ahead and I was happy that the nursery was in a separate building. The nursery was much easier to look around, it appeared to be full of Catherines, that is to say that they were all gorgeously cute, a mixture of a few in supportive seats but mostly mobile, and all were full of smiles. The nursery building offered different areas for different activities, including quiet space, and their care was wonderful. The school had their own children's nurse. This was the right place for our poorly daughter who had not seemed to fit anywhere else.

Catherine began to grow and become more settled, slept better at night (although never without waking at least once needing some intervention), enjoyed going to school and loved being at home with her family. These are the years that I am so grateful for, some of the simple pleasures such as her enjoyment of being pushed in her wheelchair outside or walking to school to collect Thomas, his running across the junior school playground shouting "Catherine" at the top of his voice and her huge smile when she recognised his voice. Catherine was happiest when being with people who included her, she loved to be involved in whatever was going on. She grew into a happy, smiley little girl.

Catherine's personality shone through her smile, she had a cheeky grin and a giggle that was infectious. Her squeaky hiccups were a source of amusement which would make us laugh, then she would laugh and soon everyone was joining in.

We were brave enough to take the whole family abroad on holiday (making sure we took details of the nearest hospital and emergency doctor with us) and we also went to stay with family. Of course, all these trips took hours of planning to make sure we had enough supplies and all essential equipment packed as well as equal amounts "just in case of illness or delay".

Over the years it became apparent that most of Catherine's problems were caused by the poor muscle tone which was a result of her brain damage. Her limbs were highly toned and she had muscle spasms causing rigid stretching of her arms and legs, and her involuntary muscles were weak which resulted in most of her problems with slow gut, digestion and bowels, and breathing difficulties.

We needed to change her position for her, she always had supportive seating but needed to lay down to stretch out and keep her joints mobile. When she was moved it would cause her whole body to spasm and become rigid, and good luck to the person who lifted her without taking this into account, she would instantly change from being chilled and relaxed into something akin to a plank of wood in your arms! This was obviously more of a challenge as she grew, and the muscle spasms became stronger. She was on several daily doses of medication to try and help control the strength of the spasms which were so uncomfortable and sometimes painful for her. As she was held, it was necessary to gently push her hips to break the spasm, she would gradually relax in your arms but at times we used to comment that it was like trying to cuddle an ironing board!

Although we never had a definitive diagnosis, Catherine had collected a list of descriptions of her disabilities and symptoms including brain damage, spastic quadriplegic cerebral palsy, oesophageal reflux, and blindness, which helped achieve intervention for each of her difficulties.

Generally, it felt as though we had found a good routine, through medication, therapy, respite and school interventions. We were feeding her just little tasters to add to a slow gastrostomy pump feed, so her stomach was never full or empty. We attended various specialist clinics to address each of her problems and her Paediatrician was responsible for co-ordinating the findings from all these consultations. One of the most helpful of our specialist clinics was the joint clinic run by Catherine's Gastroenterologist and Surgeon, both great characters who worked very well together. We saw them regularly and through them a routine was found which suited Catherine by keeping her gut moving and her digestion comfortable, involving high calorie feed, supplements, medication and suppositories. This was reviewed regularly to ensure any problems were detected early. We actually used to look forward to their clinics, they were receptive to our concerns, knowledgeable, always helpful, often amusing, and we would leave feeling supported by them.

We had equipment to help with seating, feeding, sleeping, breathing and mobility. The extent of Catherine's learning disability was now evident, and we had gradually altered our expectations accordingly.

6

SCHOOL

What wonderful places special needs schools are! The staff are kind, caring, positive, and encouraging which means their students are happy and accepting of each other, they are humbling places to be.

School was a great experience for Catherine, and when she was well she thrived there, the atmosphere was noisy and apparently chaotic with their diverse mix of children, but there was a structure which she enjoyed, and she was safe and cared for by people who understood her limitations and were able to give her the stimulation she needed.

They had all kinds of specialist equipment there to compensate for a huge variety of disabilities and if the right kit was not available, they would arrange to loan it for trial. As importantly though, they knew how to look after Catherine and what to do when she was ill. There was an efficient and skilled nurse on site who would help with care plans, communicate with me and was apparently completely unflappable! This made such a difference to me, I still received phone calls telling me Catherine was unwell, but they were calmly done, and included a plan of action, like advising that they would keep her at school and monitor her, or whether I needed to collect her and more importantly, how urgently I needed to collect her. Over the years Catherine was at school we had three school nurses, each as kind, competent and good at communicating as the last. I needed to regularly pass on changes in care so I came to know them all well.

Our Paediatrician held his clinics in the school which was so much more convenient than having to take her out of school and trek up to the hospital.

Catherine had a Statement of Special Educational Need, which is a formal document detailing a child's learning difficulties, and the help that should be given. The aim of the Statement is to make sure that the child gets the right support to enable them to make progress in school.

She started in the School nursery when she was 3 ½ and I really felt that I had got my life back. In the first few weeks I took her for some ½ day sessions and was so relieved to find I was handing over a bag of feeding equipment, dressings and medication to people who knew exactly what to do and asked all the right questions about her care.

The nursery staff were so kind and understanding, I remember dropping Catherine off one morning after a particularly bad night. She had woken several times needing medication and winding, repositioning, pad change and once when yet again (because this happened at least once a week) her feeding pump had become unattached meaning her bed was soaked with milk, dripping onto the floor. This meant she had to be lifted out, cold, wet and shivering to be put in our bed to warm up while hers was changed. It happened regularly, I was exhausted and tearful. I dropped Catherine at nursery, holding it together just long enough to handover information they needed about our interrupted night. I briefly told them that she would probably be tired and in need of a nap, and just before the tears started to fall, I left. The lovely teacher came running after me and persuaded me to go back with her for a cup of coffee and some reassurance. She was so caring (I literally cried all over her!) and seemed to totally understand my contrasting mass of emotions and expected my floods of tears, then she talked me through how they might be able to help. Some people you just have an instant rapport with, and I am still friends with Catherine's first lovely nursery teacher today.

It was also in nursery that Catherine met one of her most important friends, a delightful boy who at that time was very mobile, very jolly, often noisy, and it seems they also had an instant rapport! He was 6 months older so theoretically was in the year above but being a school with small numbers, they were in the same class much of the time and went up the key stages more or less together. Catherine loved his attention, and his loudness would make her laugh, he looked out for her and she enjoyed being with him, they were a good match.

The support of the school staff was so appreciated by us, they knew how to help us and tried to make themselves available to give advice when we asked. I also now had regular daily contact with other parents who were going through similar distressing and life changing times with uncertainty of their children's futures, and we all supported each other. As important was that I now had some time to myself whilst Catherine was in their capable hands as we had long passed a time when I could leave her with friends or family.

We were fortunate that Catherine was entitled to transport to school. Transport was funded and organised by the Local Education Authority, a wheelchair accessible bus would have a route round the local area and collect its cargo of children. The bus had a volunteer driver and a paid escort. What lovely people they were! They were both very caring, Catherine was always in attentive hands. I did worry about the sickness aspect though, as this usually involved having to vent through her gastrostomy, it was not just a question of mopping up.

One day Thomas and I were rushing up the road (there was never much time between me collecting him from school and Catherine's return home from her school by bus) and the bus came speeding along the road behind us with the horn blaring. We started running and reached the house just as the bus pulled up, the doors flew open and the driver jumped out "she's trying to be sick"! Oh dear! For Catherine though the experience of her journey to school was part of her enjoyment of the school day, the children who could, would sing, she would giggle, and everyone generally had great fun.

Catherine spent 2 years in School nursery where they managed all her needs well and supported me with organising her daily routine so they could do as many of her procedures at school as was possible. They had their own Occupational Therapist who arranged assessments for home seating, sleep system and moving and handling, and a Physiotherapist who produced programmes for chest physio and exercises to be followed in school and for us to do at home. They liaised with our Dietitian for issues with feeding.

I have huge reservations when I hear about the push for disabled children to be integrated into mainstream schools – all this expertise which was so hugely beneficial for Catherine would be diluted around all of Basingstoke's schools, and the interaction with her special friends would have been lost. She was a child who could not initiate interaction with other children and needed someone to move her wheelchair and adapt activity for her. Being in a school who would ensure she was included in all that was going on was delightful for her.

After nursery Catherine would attend the main school, which I was more familiar with now and appeared a lot less scary than that first day when we had looked around. It included all Key Stages right up to age 19, meaning that we would never have to worry about her changing school again and all the knowledge about her cares, likes and dislikes that they had built up in nursery would be passed on as she moved up the School.

Through Catherine's school, we had found a whole world we never knew existed. Her own friends were brave, characterful children who meet their challenges head on and who love unconditionally, and their families all of whom have different struggles, we have shared support and friendship. I was introduced to "ProActive Parents", a network that had been formed by local parents with common goals. Through necessity it was inclusive of children of all disabilities, and their siblings, who all played and socialised together. They had a programme of activities for the children, all accessible, for even the most disabled child, but of equal value were the evening get-togethers for the parents. A social life!

This group and our involvement with Catherine's school for Basingstoke's most severely disabled children taught us some of the greatest awareness anyone could hope for. That of understanding and not fearing disability, and total acceptance that everyone is unique and individual, and everyone has something to offer. This is one of the most positive aspects of being a special needs family, and the lessons that can be learned from these strong resilient children are endless. It was also a huge eye-opener for me, I thought as an Occupational Therapist that I understood disability but there is nothing that can teach even the most qualified health professional better than actually living that life yourself.

Within a year of Catherine joining the school I had joined the Parent & Teachers Association committee which apart from helping with fundraising gave me an opportunity to get to know some of the staff and parents better. I loved being involved in this aspect of school and really enjoyed the social side – going to the pub after meetings seemed to be almost as important as the events we were planning and I felt a real kinship with the other parents who took the opportunity to escape for a drink and chat.

The move from Nursery into Year 1 (infants) was a huge worry for me. I was concerned that the relationships I had formed with the nursery team would be lost and I would have to start again with her new teacher. I need not have worried, school were used to it. Catherine joined her new class for a few sessions at the end of her last term in nursery and I was invited to meet her new teacher, who was every bit as caring, competent and approachable as the staff in the nursery. The school nurse covered the whole school so all her knowledge of Catherine's medical needs would be passed on to all her classroom staff.

And so it was through all her Key Stages. The school would have a "moving up" assembly when each child who was moving to a new Key Stage was given a short presentation showing some of their achievements, and a folder of photos and certificates of achievement was awarded. The first of these occasions caught me unawares, what an emotional experience to see how Catherine had grown and changed, and how far she had come over her two years in nursery. I found each of these presentations more emotional than the last but at least I was prepared!

As Catherine moved through school and her development increasingly fell behind her peers, she was moved into the PMLD class (for children with profound and multiple learning difficulties). Her individual targets were similar each year, she always needed someone's hand over her hand to press a switch or move an item, she enjoyed social interaction but was not able to initiate, she could make noises but not speak, and was mobile only when someone moved her. This class though was able to give more time to her individual medical needs, physio and positioning and had a very sensory approach. Although it became apparent that Catherine would be one of the children in the School with greatest need, this realisation was gradual and school helped us adjust and supported us with any changes in her condition.

The school had a hydro-swimming pool with hoisting which Catherine could access as part of her timetable. She loved being whooshed about in the water and doing aquatic versions of her physio.

She went horse riding by having support to sit high up on a pony, enjoying the fresh air, movement, the sound of hooves and the breeze on her face. She loved all the sensory programmes on offer, like working with lights and sounds, foot spas, massages, textures and tastes. Catherine loved interactive stories, laughing when someone pounced on her and enjoyed sudden sounds and spray on her face. She certainly had all kinds of experiences through school.

They had amazing equipment including a variety of switches which would operate various electrical or digital items like a computer, music or electric fan. Any movement or ability however minimal would be encouraged and practised. We used to be amused that one of her goals each year in school was to learn to press a switch (cause and effect) she never reliably managed to do this, but it made for one of my favourite stories about school. The school inspectors were visiting the morning that Catherine's class were doing baking. She had been put in charge of pressing the switch for the food mixer and some bright spark decided to remove the lid just as the inspectors came into the classroom and I'm sure you can guess ... Catherine chose that moment to press the button by herself for the first time ever, and the cake mixture flew around the room - I'd love to believe this was intentional, she loved a drama!

When Catherine turned 11, she moved into the upper school with her own age peers which was great for her as she was back in class again with her best friend. He and the other more mobile children in this class were better able to interact with her, and share, they would give her items they thought she would like. Often when she got home from school, I would hoist her out of her chair and find all kinds of things tucked round her seat, toy cars, building bricks, squishy sensory toys, it was a voyage of discovery! When these boisterous children were in PE, Catherine would go back to spend time in the PMLD class doing her physio programme, school had worked out a timetable for her which allowed her to experience the curriculum in the most varied of ways.

When Catherine became less well, she spent more time on an Acheeva Bed. This is a 6ft long, 3ft wide piece of equipment which would enable her to lay down but that could be tilted to allow her to change position. Somehow apparently it became an unwritten rule that when moving around school she had right of way regardless of what else was happening. This was evident when Catherine was moved between classes during lunchtime. Both the hall doors would need to be opened and Catherine would sail through like a queen on a galleon, steered by two staff, one at the front and the other at the back. Catherine would be propped up against pillows for comfort and would smile graciously at the various occupants as she was guided through the busy dining room!

Towards the end of Catherine's life when she was very poorly in hospital, her teacher at the time organised for the children in her class to make voice recordings. These were presented in a box of little cards, each with a press button to hear the voice of each of Catherine's friends, for her to listen to. She loved them, she responded to the voices and noises of her friends when they were played to her, it was heart-warming to see. I was in regular contact with various members of the staff at school throughout Catherine's life and knew they would be there to assist with advice or practical help.

It was partly due to the support we were having from school that I felt confident enough to change my job again. Catherine was in a good routine during term time and although Tony was happy to work from home a couple of days a week during the holidays, we had also playscheme to help cover my workdays. Although I still enjoyed orthopaedics, changes in the way supervision and appraisal were structured across the acute NHS Trust meant each individual therapist had to produce what felt like mountains of written evidence, to show they are working at the level of their pay banding. Actually, I have always loved the non-clinical side of being an Occupational Therapist, service planning, staff supervision, team support, but the amount of extra responsibility required to meet the criteria for my banding seemed less and less feasible on the part time hours I was working. Producing a lever arch file worth of paper evidence seemed more and more arduous and pointless (oh those poor trees)! I moved from my role in the acute setting back to the Wheelchair Service where I had worked before, but which was now in a Community NHS Trust, CPD requirements done in a different way! Also the size of the team had doubled since I worked there.

7

RESPITE

When Catherine was 5 years old, and after a particularly difficult patch, our Paediatrician organised for us to have regular respite one night a week at our local NHS respite unit. At last, a night's sleep a week! But with this came all the guilt feelings most special needs parents will be familiar with, that we needed a break from the frustrations and exhaustion of looking after our poorly little daughter. I never stopped feeling sad that we needed respite, or guilty when I left her with them. Our allocation for NHS care respite was one night a week and one weekend a month. It worked so well for us, she would be collected from school on transport and go to Erdesley House (as it was then) for the night and then return to school on the bus the next morning. They told me that she was the youngest child to attend, as prior to the age of 5 it was not considered to be appropriate for a child to be away from its parents but this one night a week gave us a chance to catch up on much needed sleep, and they loved having her. We had our consultant Paediatrician to thank for this as he seemed to be able to speed through the usual slow and overcomplicated processes to get respite as soon as Catherine turned 5. Thankfully, this has changed now, it has been recognised that parents of children of any age that are equipment and medication dependent, and awake half the night, need support and respite to continue to cope.

We were lucky enough to benefit from NHS funded respite from that time onwards, and to see it go through various changes. They moved from Erdesley House which was a very grand but old and rather dilapidated building to a purpose-built facility, which was funded with combined Health and Social Services money. Tony was on the planning committee for this proposed new build, as parent representative for the children with health needs, which he found both interesting and frustrating, in equal amounts. The amount of space and funding were never going to be quite enough for the facilities required for children with complex health needs, and all the equipment that comes with them, but he did his best to champion their cause against those who were focused on the balance sheet. After all the hard-won compromises, the single storey two-sided building named Firvale was completed.

The building was divided in two, one half for children with health needs and the other half for those with social needs, and our family were honoured to be involved in the foundation bricklaying ceremony along with the parent rep for children on the Social side of the building and her family. For Catherine this was wonderful as it meant that all her friends, including her boy friend from school who had previously been to a different facility, had their "sleepovers" in the same building.

The new unit went through a long settling in period, where the manager, who was from a Social Services background, did not seem to understand any of our worries around the healthcare provision. Fortunately, before long a new manager arrived who thankfully had all the skills lacking in the old, and we really appreciated the precious nights of sleep and weekends of being able to recharge our batteries. Catherine loved her sleepovers there and in the true nature of sleepovers, generally stayed awake all night, while we were able to look forward to a whole unbroken night of sleep for ourselves. We could not have managed without this vital respite.

As well as NHS respite, we were referred to our local children's hospice, Naomi House, around the same time and although they were one of the most amazingly positive aspects of Catherine's life (especially at the end) having her accepted to be one of their children was a day of great emotion. This told us more about her life expectancy at that time than we had ever been told directly. This was a bittersweet day, to accept that we needed their support for our life limited little girl, but we also discovered that a children's hospice is not the sad place we thought it might be. Naomi House is a lively happy place, buzzing with activity, both noisy and gentle and adapted to each child's needs. They gave us an allocation of nights to use either as a break for us to stay with Catherine at the House and be pampered, or to use as respite – this gave us the opportunity to take Tom away on holidays which we could not do otherwise. They also offered support and activities for siblings; Tom went on outdoor activity days where he had a great time enjoying new experiences and being spoilt rotten!

Catherine loved her time at Naomi House; she really was treated like royalty having a spa break. We would phone each morning and evening to see how she was, once when we rang we were told she'd had a swim, followed by a hand massage and was now sitting with her feet in a bowl of lentils!

She always came home with hand & foot paintings, collages, toys and gifts.

Each year I saved a couple of days to book during the run up to Christmas. This was partly to allow time to do Christmas shopping and preparations and for Tony and I to go to a work Christmas do, but also for Catherine, because Naomi House is truly magical at Christmas. The House is covered with pretty lights and decorations, and of course the great man himself visits – he visits several times during the pre-Christmas period and often one of these visits is by helicopter! The excitement! A local Forces base provided this, and it was one of the most magical events for the children and their families.

In fact, it was during this time which was coming up to Christmas, I had the pleasure of meeting Santa! He was off-duty in his jeans, and popped in to visit us in our room, he asked me what Catherine would like for Christmas – his official visit was to be the next day and, as Catherine was supposed to have gone home by now, she was not on his present list. All I could come up with on the spur of the moment was some warm socks, she suffers with cold feet. His face was a picture, after hesitating he said "we have a bigger budget than that" so I came up with a few other probably not very helpful suggestions. He arrived the next day, this time in the red suit, he brought had REAL baby reindeer with him. They had built a beautiful grotto for him outside, lit with fairy lights in the garden, we could see from our room. It was truly magical. Catherine was too poorly to go out and see him, so he came to see us in her room and gave her a whole sack full of perfect presents (including warm socks!) It was very moving. It seems that the fundraising for Christmas presents is very generous, but as important for us was that Catherine was made to feel special and spoilt at a time when she was struggling.

One of the differences with our Naomi House respite is that they also had accommodation for parents to stay with their child. When Catherine was little, Thomas and I would stay with her (Tony usually stayed at home to work), it was such a treat to be able to be with her but not be responsible for the medical and nursing side of her care, I could just be her Mum. Thomas also enjoyed these breaks, he loved the playroom, up to date games and gaming consoles, the well-stocked music room and choice of DVDs as well as having the opportunity to share all these with Catherine.

Their facilities are state of the art and over the 9 years that we were a Naomi House family, we tried most of them. We did not think at the time that we were building memories, but now I look back I can remember so many lovely occasions we enjoyed real quality time together. Thomas would wheel her off into the music room and proceed to bash away on the drums with her alternately jumping out of her skin or shrieking with laughter. They went in the hydro pool together and outside in the garden with Catherine on the wheelchair swing, they enjoyed the sensory room with its heated waterbed, light display and soothing music.

But really the most remarkable thing about Naomi House from my point of view was the expertise and caring of the clinical team. There was nothing they did not cope with, any deterioration in Catherine's condition was accompanied by more specialist equipment, new techniques in care and extra responsibility but they were able to meet all these needs.

Towards the end of her life Catherine spent more time at Naomi House, now called Naomi House & Jacksplace, as it had expanded to cater for young adults. She was having more hospital admissions and her gradual deterioration in condition needed greater levels of care. After she was diagnosed with an upper respiratory collapse, where her muscle tone was too weak to keep her airway open, she had a permanent tube placed through her nose and down into her windpipe, (naso-pharyngeal airway) which required regular suctioning, cleaning, taping to her face and replacing weekly. They helped us leave hospital after a difficult hospital admission, by providing a "step down" which means we could come home via the hospice, after a couple of nights with them when they nurtured and supported us to cope with new equipment and changes in her care.

All our respite nights at Firvale and Naomi House were precious nights of sleep for us. I felt that we looked forward to respite like thirsty people needing water! People used to ask us what we were planning to do on our respite night – well, sleep of course! We honestly felt that no-one understood how sleep deprived we were, we were up at least twice a night throughout Catherine's life, but often more and may involve changing her bed, and her, which often become wet with feed or leakage from her gastrostomy or nappy/pad, but always to at least reposition her, wind her or give her meds through her gastrostomy. I am sure people thought we exaggerated our exhaustion. I know that unless people have experienced a full-time caring role themselves, with all the attached accountability, they cannot begin to understand how the slow and insidious responsibility takes over your own life and goals.

8

PARENT OR NURSE?

Of course, time doesn't stand still, and Catherine was growing and developing. With her growth came new problems associated with her development and size. By the time she was aged 10, although still small for her age, we started to struggle with manual handling, especially endless trips up and down stairs several times a day with equipment and carrying Catherine up and down, a manoeuvre which was becoming increasingly unsafe.

Access had also become an issue, although we only had one step at the front door, it was just the wrong size to get all four wheelchair wheels on, and now

Catherine was in a seating system, the whole kit was heavy. We had a Social Services OT involved who assessed this and advised on an elaborate system of ramping at the front door by removing a flower bed and having a permanent structure which would need to be about 4 metres long – even though I had just asked for a half step. I thought this would be a great temporary measure to help me to get the wheelchair in and out of the house. She didn't agree though I explained that we planned to move to a bungalow as soon as we could find the right one. I just did not feel it justified a permanent ramp when we hoped to move in a few months. My Dad rescued us again! He made the most perfect wooden step extension, and the problem was solved. I resolved I would never be that OT! It is so important to listen to what your patients/relatives are saying to you, what a waste of resources it would have been to put in a permanent ramp and would not have helped us sell the house.

After a long search we found the right bungalow. We needed to do some alterations so Catherine was able to have a bedroom next to ours. This meant we could hear her at night and get to her quickly when she needed intervention and we had hoisting installed in bathroom and bedroom. Being on one level made a difference from day one, no more running up and down stairs, and all her equipment was easily moved between rooms. Seemingly small things like a covered entry porch made a huge difference to us, it was big enough to shelter the whole wheelchair plus equipment whilst unloading the rest of the kit from the car. The hall is straight and wide, again perfect for Catherine in her wheelchair with her many, many bags!

We started to have to make decisions about orthopaedic intervention, like surgery to her hips to reduce her leg scissoring, and whether her spinal kyphosis (curvature) needed support. Her orthopaedic surgery to release the tendons in her hips was one of the most negative experiences we had of all her hospital admissions. The Orthopaedic ward where Catherine was treated was not equipped to cope with her learning difficulty, muscle tone or feeding problems. We were there for orthopaedics only. This became evident as she was being clerked in, all her medications were detailed on her meds chart but I was asked several times during this process why her drugs could not be given together, so they were not spread out so much during the day. I could see it was inconvenient for them, but I thought it should have been obvious that her routine had been carefully worked out for the best effect.

I tried to explain about the importance of positioning and care of her gastrostomy, but I did not see this noted down anywhere. I realised I could not leave her at all, I did my usual thing of making friends with the mums of other children in the bay so I could at least go to the toilet or have a shower, when I would ask them to keep an eye and ring Catherine's buzzer to attract nursing attention if she was unsettled. I was required to do all her cares, feeds, and to remind the staff when her medication was due. It was always late and sometimes so late that she was due the next dose of the same drug. We were required to provide all Catherine's usual medications on admission to hospital, but they would take them away to keep safe. This meant they were locked in the drug cupboard and needed constant reminding when each dosage was due. I obviously understand the need for locking meds away, but there really needs to be a system for children on high levels of medication to be able to access it. Catherine was dependent on all her meds and it was so frustrating that I felt the whole admission was spent chasing up routine medication.

Despite 2 weeks of traction, the surgery on the tendons in her hips failed, and she was back to square one within a month. The surgery was intended to prevent her crossing her legs which was putting her hips at risk of dislocation. Despite the tendon release, her muscle tone was so strong that the surgery made little difference.

When her back developed a marked kyphosis, I was adamant that she would not have surgery if there were non-surgical options. Also, working again for the Wheelchair Service meant regularly doing seating clinics to provide postural support, sometimes for young people who have had failed back surgery. I knew from experience that back surgery to correct spinal posture does not always go well and complications can be very difficult to manage.

We still had emergency admissions for chest infections, but they became less. Now she would become poorly with skin infections or granuloma round her gastrostomy button. The mechanism for holding in a child's gastrostomy button in place is a water-filled balloon inside the stomach. Catherine's high muscle tone would increase when very upset or distressed and she was able to eject her button from her stomach with the water filled balloon still intact. I was so shocked the first time this happened. I noticed her gastrostomy button lying on the floor, still attached to the extension tube, in an expanding puddle of milk slowly soaking into the carpet. Milk was still being pumped through the tube. She had a large wet patch on the front of her T shirt where her stomach contents were leaking out of the now empty and open hole in her abdomen.

This became a regular occurrence, and caused her skin to become sore and infected, she had many hospital admissions, and we had a cupboard brimming with different creams and dressings. Over time she trialled a variety of makes of gastrostomy.

Regardless of the improvement in her frequency of sickness after her stomach surgery, she was still able to be sick (which was not supposed to happen) and it was decided to change feeding method to a trans-gastro-jejunostomy. This is where a tube would be passed through her stomach and out of the lower valve to feed her via a second narrower tube directly into her gut. It was another disaster story. The tube needed a whole new level of care because it gave access to the lower gut all interventions needed to be sterile involving gloves, dressings and sterile water flushes. It was a narrow gauge and would block up with some of the thicker medications she was on, or be pulled or dislodged from her gut, involving an emergency dash back down the motorway to Southampton radiology department where it needed to be replaced under Xray. It seemed a very flawed design as the jejunostomy tube was easily pulled out of the gastrostomy tube, particularly during any kind of movement like hoisting or even getting washed or dressed.

It soon became apparent that we had just swapped one problem for another and with agreement of her surgeon, we reverted to feeding directly into her stomach again via gastrostomy, by pump. She coped with this at a much slower rate over a longer period of about 12 hours, which meant Catherine never had a full stomach and this seemed to help the sickness.

This period has given me one of my favourite stories about the expertise at Naomi House Hospice though. During the time when we were caring for Catherine with her jejuno-tube, due to the level of care and specialism required, we were told our NHS respite unit had not had the training to look after her, so our respite with them was stopped until they had all been given the right kind of training. We were now reliant on Naomi House for our respite but had two bookings in a row cancelled due to their needing our bed for a child at the end of life.

We were exhausted and in desperate need of a break so when we finally were offered a long weekend with them, Catherine went to Naomi House and we went away for a weekend to Dorset. The phone signal was unreliable, in fact, non-existent in most of the places we went apart from our hotel. We went out for a walk one morning, up to the top of a steep hill with a series of masts on top (presumably including a mobile phone mast) and my phone suddenly came alive with messages. Catherine's tube was blocked and the hospice Clinical team, not able to reach us, had contacted her surgeon in Southampton for advice. They needed us know that if they could not clear the tube they would arrange for her transfer to hospital. I phoned straight away but in the time between their messages and my call they told me they had managed to unblock it. What a relief! We carried on with our weekend so grateful for the caring and expertise of the Naomi House doctor and nurses and the fact that they had been prepared to arrange her transfer to hospital themselves and for her to be accompanied by someone with the right skills.

As her main carer, I gradually learned skills in all aspects of this extremely challenging job. I started to draw up my own drug charts as she was on 14 or so different drug dosages a day, all needing to be drawn up or mixed and administered by gastrostomy, jejunostomy, spacer or nebuliser. These drug charts were essential. I can't think how anyone would safely manage without them, when so many interventions are needed a day it would be impossible to keep a track. Also, when more than one person is responsible for giving medication it is even more important to mark when it has been done.

When she came home after a period of being in hospital, we inevitably had courses of antibiotics and puffers to add into the mix. Stocks of medication needed to be checked and ordered from our GP surgery (more recently we were able to do online prescriptions) and collected from the pharmacy. Her gastrostomy supplies came with the feed, extension tubes, giving sets and flexitainers from whichever laboratory was being used by our Trust at the time. Later Catherine required oxygen which came from a different company, so we had a large (noisy) oxygen machine called a concentrator which sat out in the hall with enough tubing to reach all necessary rooms in the bungalow, as well as oxygen cylinders both large and portable. Her nebulisers had a specialist filter and then much later her naso-pharyngeal airway was replaced weekly, we had a non-invasive ventilator and all the disposables needed for that. All these supplies had to be ordered and monitored along with basic stuff like nappies or pads and wipes.

Whenever we went anywhere, even just a walk down the road, a bag had to be packed with the right supplies. These bags got bigger and bigger over time, with more and more medical supplies, as her health needs grew.

As soon as things started to settle down, something new came along to worry us. I felt as though I really had changed from being a carer into a nurse. It was sometimes as though my head would explode with the amount of information I had to remember, and decisions we needed to make, it became really difficult to answer anyone who said "how are you?" so of course, we would just reply "fine thanks". It was impossible to explain how Catherine was (where do you start anyway?) and we often found it too exhausting and emotional to even try. I felt I was living a double life where I would try my best to show the face of being happy, in control and interested in the world whilst my mind was constantly on what needed to be done next with Catherine's care or worrying about the latest series of events.

9

EQUIPMENT

Our home gradually filled up with equipment. Once we had moved into our lovely bungalow, we were able to make more permanent arrangements for moving and handling. We had hoisting installed in Catherine's bedroom and the bathroom across the hall from her, which was arranged by our Social Services OT (yes, the same one who I had disagreed with during the ramping discussion a couple of years before) but this was ideal in our new home. At the time the hoist went in, it was partly for future proofing, we were still mainly lifting Catherine and felt that this was really something she enjoyed. One of the things that made us sad was that as she grew, so the amount of physical contact with her carers became less, she was hoisted in school, hospital, respite and playscheme. We were told by one of our Community professionals that it was not in Catherine's best interests that we were still lifting her. I bit my tongue, she clearly has not spent much time out and about in the world of children with disabilities, there are so many occasions when lifting is the only option, often in hospital, her ideal world does not exist!

Some of the most crucial equipment over Catherine's life was her seating. She was assessed her first buggy aged around 4 years. This rule has changed now but at that time children under 4 could not be issued with seating as it was stated that all children are in buggies up until this point. Luckily, it is now recognised that correct positioning from a young age is crucial to their posture later in life. Being the OT that I am, I had made a few small cushions to place in her buggy to ensure her spine was supported, but her first Wheelchair Service buggy made life so much more comfortable for her. It was great, the seat could be detached from the buggy base and fixed on a low frame, so she was at the same height as us when we were sitting in the living room.

Over the years we had all kinds of wheelchairs and seating in a range of Catherine's lovely bright colours, and I am pleased that they helped keep her spine straight for as long as possible.

We have been so grateful for the local provision funded by Social Services, the Hampshire Equipment Store (it has had various names over the years but that is its current title) who are able to loan equipment long term, in other words, for as long as we needed it. Over the years we were loaned various equipment for Catherine, generally recommended by our OT who would arrange for each item to be whisked away and replaced by a larger one as she grew out of things or were promptly adjusted or repaired when they needed to be.

We had loan of all kinds of adjustable comfy chairs, highchairs, chairs with wheels, chairs without wheels, bed with sleep system and cot sides, suction machine, nebuliser, and all kinds of smaller items for positioning and pressure relief. We always found the Service helpful and once when we had an emergency with one of Catherine's suction machines, another was delivered to us the same day.

The downside to all this is that it requires a certain amount of understanding or skill to use equipment safely and effectively. I know from my professional life what a difference it makes, for example, if you use all the profiling elements of an electrically adjustable bed to maximum effect. My time working in the Wheelchair Service reinforced the importance of accurate adjustment of equipment to support posture and help keep the body in a good position. This also has the effect of helping support the body systems too, and Catherine sleeping with her upper body in a slightly elevated position would help reduce her reflux, and the knee bend in the bed would stop her sliding down.

It became another extension of our caring role when handing Catherine over to anyone who would be looking after her, that we also had to know they had good understanding of how and when to use her equipment, or would need to teach them ourselves. I am often frustrated by my patients who have been issued expensive and individually adjusted equipment and then do not use it correctly, or even do not use it at all.

Equipment failures were one of my biggest irritations. Over the years the plastics for Catherine's feeding pump improved but at the start of her pump use, the tubes were connected by pushing one end into the other. These ends would part company often causing feed to be dripped on the floor, in her bed, along the pavement, in the car, you name it! One time we left a trail of milk along Southsea waterfront, along a main road near us (it dried up and was there for months) and spent many times in the middle of the night mopping up the floor under her bed. If we did not find the leak early enough, we were then dealing with an enormous puddle.

Catherine's BiPAP** machine never had the right sized mask, I know it is possible to be between sizes but the failure of this meant the seal would be lost and the machine would bleep. As she was mainly needing this support at night, this was another thing we lost sleep to.

Not all of Catherine's equipment was large or difficult to use, one of our favourite special issues was her wonderful brightly coloured boots. From a very young age it was recommended that her feet needed to be kept in a good position to prevent deformity and hopefully enable her to weight-bear. We attended an orthotic appointment where her feet were measured, and we were offered a choice of colours of tiny ankle boots with supportive insoles. We chose red. These boots became part of her trademark colourful wardrobe and varied through red, purple and pink. For a short while we were told she could not be issued with them anymore as she was not mobile. I was sorry for her as not only were they really comfortable, but they had become part of her wardrobe. Also, it seemed to me to be a real false economy, although she never walked, Catherine used a standing frame at school, and needed to have her feet secured in her wheelchair to give a good seating position. So I started to buy her boots myself online, I found Kickers do a fabulous range of multi-coloured children's Lego ankle boots, seemingly as supportive as her special boots had been. She wore these for a couple of years until our new Orthopaedic surgeon decided that she needed made to measure boots again and we went back to special issue bright boots.

Catherine never travelled light. This meant that all arrivals and departures to and from school apparently required the services of at least two adults, especially when her extra-large pink overnight suitcase travelled with her. School reported that they were always delighted when Catherine managed to get home or to respite, and back again, with everything she needed with her.

10

HOLIDAYS

One of our best ways of getting away from day-to-day stresses was to go away for a few days. Catherine loved holidays! Holidays involved all her favourite things including sunshine, being outside in the fresh air, being with family and in particular, spending quality time all together as a family. Actually, Catherine was just as happy to have days out as a holiday, but not in the cold and rain which is the disadvantage to living in England!

The logistics of going on holidays were a huge challenge. As we do not have any family who live nearby, even visiting relations meant at least staying over for one night as Catherine would not manage the amount of travelling involved in a day trip. I counted these visits as holidays, where everything needed careful planning, and they were loved by Catherine who enjoyed family time. These breaks took days of organising.

I compiled a series of packing lists which I used for holidays with all of us, and a different list for respite when Catherine would go on her own. Before leaving home, I gathered the packing together, included making sure we had enough feed and medication, but also supplies of plastics, syringes, nappies, dressings and spare gastrostomy button and NP airway tubes. We had larger equipment like her feeding pump, suction machine, nebuliser, neck brace, and of course her wheelchair with seating system as well as, oh yes, clothes! Towards the end of Catherine's life we also took oxygen away with us, or if we were going somewhere in the county of Hampshire we could arrange to have it delivered.

We also worried about where Catherine would sleep whilst we were away, as she used to wake several times a night, so we needed her to be near to us. She had her profiling bed at home with sleep system to support her and ensure her head and shoulders were slightly elevated to prevent aspirating reflux. We obviously had to improvise with her bed when we were away, using pillows and cushions, but we had to have a plug socket next to her for the pump to be charged overnight, and access to a sink to wash syringes and bottles and prepare feeds and medication. Once she became too heavy to carry upstairs, we needed to sleep downstairs. All in all, going away anywhere needed careful planning, and we always arrived with Catherine in urgent need of a change of position (lying down) and winding. What made it all worthwhile was that Catherine loved these occasions, and in particular, doting family love. Her cousins used to love Catherine cuddles and she loved their attention.

Holidays abroad took months of planning. All the above supplies needed but for a whole week. Catherine would have an enormous suitcase to herself and the rest of the family would share one! I used to ask our paediatrician to write a letter with a summary of Catherine's health problems in case she needed to be hospitalised whilst we were away, which his secretary would then translate into either Spanish or Portuguese depending on where we were going. I believe she used a translation app on the computer, but still impressive! We also had to have a letter for airport security to explain why Catherine was attached to a bottle of formula which contained more than 100 mls.

We took Catherine on holiday abroad, which was lovely and worth all the effort beforehand. I have lots of memories especially of one holiday in Portugal where we spent half the holiday with Tony's Mum and sister and half with my parents.

Although my memories of these holidays also include some of the things that made us stand apart and feel so different as a family, one flight had so many ridiculous things go wrong it became funny. Like trying to get through security with bottles of liquid medication after rules about taking liquid on aeroplanes became stricter, Catherine was attached to her feeding pump carrying 1 litre of feed. Despite having a letter from our Paediatrician explaining what the bottle contained, I really thought they were going to make us throw it away and Catherine would have gone without feed for several hours.

Beforehand I had arranged with the airline for a special seat to be put in her plane seat to give extra support, but we had to leave her wheelchair and seating system at the bottom of the plane steps. The only way to get her into the plane was for Tony to carry her up the steps whilst I walked close behind with her feeding pump, and poor young Tom was left carrying the hand luggage whilst the cabin crew stood at the top of the steps watching. When we landed the other end, Tom was looking out of the plane window and said "Oh look Mum, there's Catherine's buggy", he was right, there it was sitting on top of the luggage truck full of suitcases heading into the terminal! It was too late for anyone to stop it and we were stranded on the plane. We waited half an hour whilst they found an adult wheelchair which I sat in with Catherine on my lap, Tony and Tom carrying her equipment and many bags. We were reunited with her wheelchair and suitcases in the terminal.

On the return flight they had omitted to put the special seat for her in the plane and it really looked as though they might offload us. The Captain was called and we were relieved that we convinced him we could wedge her into her plane seat between Tony and I using pillows and blankets. They were actually suggesting the plane should go back to the UK without us and return 8 hours later with the seat in place. What a disaster that would have been.

I took the children abroad on my own once. I am still proud of this achievement! We went to Disneyland Paris to meet and stay with friends of ours who have a time share there. This is my friend who used to be Catherine's school nurse, so, a perfect holiday partner. They also have a young person with special needs (a child at the time of this trip) and his brother both of whom Catherine and Thomas had great relationships with. But again, all the careful planning in the world could not cover every eventuality. This time it was snow. We were to go over the October half term and come the day of travel we woke up to a blanket of thick snow, and it was still snowing. We were catching the Eurostar from Ashford and Catherine had been at respite the night before to allow me time to pack everything and load the car. Tom and I got up at 5.00 am and went to collect Catherine. Already the estate where Firvale respite unit is, was deep in snow. However, I was not going to be deterred! With the help of the respite staff, I loaded her into the car and were on our way with the radio telling me that driving was treacherous, and people should not travel unless they had to. By the time we were on the M20 driving towards Ashford the visibility was through driving snow and we were lucky to be doing 40 mph.

I had allowed plenty of time for the journey, but we were fast running out. We arrived at the carpark and made a mad dash for the train. Of course, we needed special assistance which involved checking-in at a special check-in desk, all time-consuming. We caught the train with about 5 minutes to spare, in fact, I think we were the last people to board. What a stressful start to what was a lovely holiday. We met our friends the other end and we had a fabulous time.

Both children enjoyed the holiday although the Disneyland experience for Tom was completely different to Catherine's. He was really in his element with all the rides, figures, shops and general excitement of the place. For Catherine though, it was very cold (although not snowing) and she spent very long periods in her chair, even though we had fast-passes there were still long queues for the rides, most of which she could not access. But again, the experience of being on holiday with family and friends was the thing Catherine enjoyed most, and for me, being away with friends who could help to look after her was lovely.

Despite the weeks of holiday organising, of course the one thing we could not plan was Catherine's health. One holiday when she was 5, we had planned to go to Portugal with my parents, but the week before, Catherine was admitted to Basingstoke hospital with an infection, this time in the skin around her gastrostomy which was making her very ill.

During the course of that week, she did not pick up at all and it became obvious that she was not going to be able to go on holiday. After discussions between ourselves and the doctors, we decided that Tom and I would go away with Mum and Dad (who had not been abroad for some years due to my Dad's deteriorating health) and Tony would stay at home with Catherine.

We naively assumed that she would improve. Poor Mum and Dad, as the plane took off, I burst into tears, I found it unbearable to be jetting off away from our poorly Catherine. I tried my best not to let Tom see how worried I was about her, but the holiday became increasingly difficult. Every time I rang home, the only news was bad. Catherine's condition was deteriorating. I phoned home every day (before mobile phones, I had to walk down into the local village to the phone box) and hope Tony was home to speak to. After 4 days he told me the doctors had decided she needed to be in the care of her Gastric Surgeon who was in Southampton. She was transferred by ambulance to the children's surgical ward where she had her gastrostomy button taken out to allow the infected area to heal and the gastrostomy hole to reduce, and she was back to having an NG tube for feeding instead.

I wanted to be home with her so Tony and I agreed he would fly out to Portugal to be with Tom and I would come home, so we had brief few hours handover in Portugal and I flew back. How glad I was to be able to be reunited with her, and once in the specialist care of the Surgeon she slowly improved.

The other memory of that particular hospital admission was that we were having a new bathroom fitted at home, of course, the idea was that this was to be done whilst we were on holiday and we would come home to our fabulous new bathroom. Ah well, the best laid plans, and all that! At least Tom and Mum and Dad had been able to have their holiday and Tony and I, half each! I am very glad that we still went on the holiday as this was the last time that my parents went abroad together as my Dad died the following year of the COPD he had been struggling with for years.

Catherine also went on holiday without us. She was lucky enough to be invited for a week in Lourdes with a marvellous group of people known as the HCPT (Hosanna House and Children's Pilgrimage Trust). They are a United Kingdom based Catholic charity which travels with disabled and disadvantaged children on pilgrimage to Lourdes, France.

We were contacted by our local group after a referral from Naomi House and through our priest at Tony's church in Basingstoke. He knew the group well as he had previously been priest in a church in Southampton where this group are based, and he knew our family well enough to think Catherine would really enjoy going. Their group doctor phoned me and explained what they are about and said they would like to offer Catherine a fully funded holiday with them. We were pretty dumbstruck by the idea! Firstly, how they would manage to look after all Catherine's needs and secondly by the generosity of the group who were not even asking for a donation towards the holiday, I honestly felt we were not worthy.

They came to meet Catherine and talk to us. Their group based in Southampton had several doctors and nurses amongst their helpers and because of that were particularly looking to support children with health needs. Following a few meetings for them to get to know Catherine and her care plan, she went away with them for a week at Easter.

We took her to the meeting point, handed them all her bags, supplies and a pirate outfit(!) and off she went in the coach. It felt so strange to be waving her off for a week away without us. True to our form we took the opportunity to go away ourselves but were able to follow her progress with her wonderful group of carers on their HCPT website. We went to the internet café in our hotel and logged on to see what she had been doing each day. She had such an enjoyable time with them with all kinds of unique experiences. They coped with all her cares and routines, including keeping a watch over her at night. We are so glad we were brave enough to let her have this extraordinary and spiritual experience, and grateful that they were brave enough to take her.

We were proud of how well travelled Catherine was but as her equipment dependency grew, we decided to find a holiday home closer to our own home and bought a small two bedroomed bungalow in a holiday village on the quiet west coast of the Isle of Wight.

We had many, many, fabulous holidays and short breaks there, this suited us much better as we would leave supplies at the beginning of each season for Catherine which eased the packing somewhat, and the local hospital has links with Southampton General, so any health emergency would be easier too. We loved the ferry journey and could be in our holiday place a little more than a couple of hours after leaving home.

We went for a week during Catherine's last summer, just before her 14th birthday, by this time she was oxygen dependent and our oxygen supplier would deliver direct to our IOW bungalow which meant when we arrived, the concentrator and cylinders were already there. The weather was beautiful, and we spent most of the time outside in the sunshine. She was able to be in her wheelchair outside for her twice daily nebulisers, or in the shade, on the beach, watching us playing mini golf or just pottering around the grounds. Catherine sat smiling in her wheelchair, loving the breeze on her face and just being outside with her family. My happy smiling photos are testament to a wonderful last holiday for her.

11

CHRISTMAS

I was lucky to have been brought up in a family who enjoyed every aspect of Christmas and embraced the whole thing. From the preparations beforehand like shopping, putting up decorations and enjoying pre-Christmas parties, to the actual day including going to church and our family time. Growing up, relations from both sides of my family lived within a few miles of each other in North London so we were able to share this lovely time together.

Unfortunately, this is no longer the case for us, as living in Basingstoke, we are not near any of our wider family. Tony has always worked long hours in his busy accountancy practice, often including evenings and weekends and his busiest time of year is in the winter months leading up to submitting client's tax returns at the end of January. In fact, just about the time all the Christmas preparations start.

Also of course, winter is the time when all the cold and flu bugs arrive with a vengeance and poor Catherine always caught the lot. She generally had at least one hospital admission before the beginning of December and she was 7 years old before we managed to have a whole Christmas and New Year period without spending some of it in hospital. I got into the habit of starting our Christmas shopping in July as I knew that by November my time would be spent looking after a poorly Catherine. As much as people say everyone understands how difficult it is to have a child in hospital, my experience tells me that they still expect Christmas/birthday cards and presents (one year I bought them all in the Southampton hospital shop!).

Sadly, I started to dread Christmas. Tony would have his huge work pressures which left me with all the shopping and preparations for Christmas itself, whilst trying to be in hospital for our poorly Catherine. Added to that, we had the pressure of travelling between Basingstoke, London and the Midlands to celebrate Christmas with family. And of course, it being the middle of winter the weather is always cold and wet, or worse when you are travelling, snowy. One Christmas we decided we needed to do our visiting to the Midlands differently as Catherine had really become too heavy to carry upstairs plus she had so much equipment with her we thought it would be better to divide our family. She and I stayed with my brother (who lives about 45 mins away from Tony's Mum) and Tony and Tom stayed with his Mum. The weather was appalling and travelling between the two houses was difficult enough but then came the heavy snow. One day, having gone out to meet up, we watched dismayed as thick snow fell, it looked as though we might not be able to get back to the house where all Catherine's medication and pump feed supplies were. It was clear that the whole Christmas period was going to have to be celebrated at home from now on.

One year (before the decision to be at home) we had left my parents in London the day after Boxing Day and started our journey to Tony's family in the Midlands, we were already worried about Catherine's spiking temperature and worsening cough; we had just got onto the M25 when she had a prolonged period of coughing and retching, we looked at each other and knew we needed to change our plans and head home. We were back in Basingstoke and Catherine was admitted to the Paediatric Ward by lunchtime.

Some of these difficult times had lighter moments too though. That particular admission was deemed to be caused by yet another virus, but nothing too serious, it seemed Catherine just needed intravenous fluids, oxygen, antibiotics and rest. We decided Tony should take Thomas and go to up to his Mum in the Midlands as originally planned for the few days to New Year. I stayed behind with Catherine. On New Year's Eve I was sitting in her cubicle with her, she was in an oxygen head box, still poorly, and I was reading quietly, I was sure I could hear Thomas. Then I heard lots of giggling and shushing at the same time our young Thomas came hurtling into the room – Tony had planned that they would surprise us but Tom couldn't wait! It was lovely; they came back in time for us to celebrate New Year together.

As Catherine grew and became more settled though, Christmas took on a more magical appearance. She loved all the pretty lights and singing, well, all the fuss really. We went to the Winter Wonderland at Paulton's Park with the ProActive Parents group one year; we were walking through the beautifully animated winding path to Santa's grotto which included passing under a tunnel of twinkling fairy lights, Catherine's face was an absolute picture of joy, it was wonderful. Of course, Thomas also loved these experiences too and it was delightful to share it with everyone. I liked to put up lights outside our house which Catherine loved, I'm not sure Thomas was that fussed but I really enjoyed the look of our road with ours' and our neighbours' Christmas lights. I still put up Christmas lights outside and they are now referred to by us and our neighbours as Catherine's lights.

Catherine was always in the Christmas nativity, as all the children in the school were, but as anyone who has ever been to a nativity in a special school will know, these occasions are unbelievably moving. I was every bit as proud when she was Rudolph as I was when she was Mary!

One Autumn term her teacher had been doing lots of work with Catherine and another girl in her class using interactive equipment involving a beam of light which when crossed would cause a sound to be heard (known as Soundbeam). They needed to lift their heads and move their hands across the beam to be rewarded with an array of beautiful sounds. She was doing very well at this during their rehearsals, so it was decided as Christmas approached to showcase this in the Christmas concert. There would be a group of children playing bells, more on boomwhackers (percussion) and Catherine and her co-star friend were headlined to show off their skills on the Soundbeam. The great day arrived, and we were advised to bring a box of tissues for our daughter's special appearance and what happened? Both girls went to sleep! No amount of shaking, coaxing and calling could wake them!

Christmas day itself was always challenging even when Catherine was well. She had her medicine and feeding regime, we always had a traditional turkey dinner with all the trimmings, and we went to church. A busy day but it was really lovely to share this time at home together, the four of us. Rather late on, in fact only the last couple of years, I realised it was a really good idea to have a couple of hours of help from a carer on Christmas day. And that amazingly there are carers who are agreeable to working that day. This gave Catherine some pamper time as she was helped into her finery and had her nails done, leaving me free to cook the turkey. I was so grateful to our lovely carer who was prepared to come in on Christmas day, she will never know what a difference she made to me.

12

FRIENDS

I am lucky that I lived in the same part of North London for all my childhood, and even when I left home and moved away, my parents still lived in the same house where I had grown up, and loved me to visit. I still have friends who I have known most of my life. In fact my friend that I went travelling with I have known all my life – our Mums were pregnant at the same time and we were born within 3 weeks of each other (me first as she's happy to remind me!). They have all left London now, but we are still in touch (oh the power of Facebook!) and I love the fact that they have known me through all phases of my life. We meet when we can, but rarely, and it is so good to see them, we always have so much to catch up on. There is a real comfort in knowing they are there, and we still keep in touch with messages.

Contrast to that, it would be difficult to describe the instant common bond that I have felt when I met another parent with a disabled child. So much is unspoken but understood and the need for giving and receiving support is strong. These friendships feel different as they all start with a basic understanding of the real challenges in our lives. I like to think we support each other equally and I know that all of us at different times have been struggling more or less than the others.

There are lots of occasions I can think of where the kindness of friends has been so special. One of our closest friends and Catherine's Godmother, who was a nurse at our local Hospice next to Basingstoke hospital, would come to visit us on the children's ward after she had finished her shift. She would arrive with a big smile, coffee for me and loving care for Catherine, it was so good to have adult company and for Catherine to have visitors.

We had a few regular visitors and really looked forward to seeing them and hearing all about what is going on in the outside world – being in hospital is like being in a cocoon where your lives revolve around fear for your poorly child, feeling a frightening lack of control and having urgent decisions to be made about care. Time passes unbearably slowly and it really feels as though time stands still, news from outside is always a surprise, is life really carrying on without us?

Our hospital visitors were very much appreciated, I know it's quite hard work visiting people in hospital; the parking is designed to put you off before you start but it is so lovely to see a friendly face peering round the door!

I knew I had found the right profession when I realised I also have that same instant bond with my therapy colleagues. We share a similar outlook and sense of humour, the importance of which cannot be understated when it comes to support through difficult times. At times I had to leave work in a hurry to be with Catherine, one time I remember in particular when I was called out of a clinic to take a phone call. Southampton HDU were calling to say that Catherine's blood pressure was unstable and they were suggesting I should come to be with her quickly. I left immediately and one of my wheelchair Occupational Therapy colleagues was kind enough to step in and cover my clinic. This was so kind, it would have been easy to cancel them and put them back on the waiting list but her kindness meant they had their appointment and I did not have to bear the burden of letting people down.

Catherine's own friends were many, from school and play schemes, and because of their varied range of ages, abilities and disabilities, they all had so much to offer. Catherine loved attending the playscheme which was run in school through the holidays, it was staffed by some of the school teaching staff, plus young helpers. The scheme came to an end, which was a real worry for us. The six-week summer holiday is a long time for a child who is not able to entertain themselves, see their friends or interact with others without support.

We were introduced to a new organisation, Challengers. They started originally in Guildford but were just introducing a new playscheme in Basingstoke, their mission to provide truly inclusive, fun and safe places for all disabled children to spend time with their friends, was ideal for Catherine.

They are a such good organisation who offered the perfect solution to provide somewhere for Catherine to go during the holidays whilst I was working, and gave her all the stimulation and fun she could handle! Their young carers would support every child even those only able to join in a minimal way, to do cooking, painting, going out for walks, watching movies, playing games and reading stories. She loved this interaction with her friends, and through their holistic approach, meant there were children from other local special schools too, an opportunity to make more friends. Most of the staff are young themselves, which is great for the children, but one of the most important aspects for us is that they were happy to learn how to manage Catherine's equipment, feeds, medication and suction machine. She enjoyed going and always came home full of smiles.

Catherine loved to have human contact, she was a very tactile girl and was never happier than when she was being cuddled. I am sure she became a rugby lover for this reason! She would recognize the introduction music to the Six Nations or Rugby World Cup with a beaming smile, this meant she would get to have a cuddle with her Dad. One of Tony's friends (who is actually the Dad of our lovely young carer mentioned in the next chapter) often came over to watch the games, and Catherine would happily receive cuddles and attention, jumping with the loud cheering and banter. She did not mind which team won she was as happy whoever it was!

It is recognised that caring can be very isolating partly of course due to the fact that going out is difficult, both with and without the person for whom you are caring. Our regular carers learned about Catherine's routine by sharing tasks with me, but finding skilled carers to sit for an evening when we were not there was more of an issue. This made it a real challenge for both Tony and I to go out for an evening together. It was almost more trouble than it was worth! One New Year's Eve we both went to the same party but separately, I went to the first half of the party and came home at 11.15, Tony then went for midnight celebrations and afterwards.

I used to have to start planning our evenings out way in advance, making sure Catherine's supplies were topped up, the care plan, routine, and medication charts were left for the carer along with all the meds bottles, nebulisers, etc. As one of our carers will testify, I managed to have the oxygen adaptor and tubing attached to a nearly empty cylinder, eek, I forgot to check before going out. Luckily, she was fully competent enough to notice and switch cylinders but has reminded me of it many times since!

The arrival of social media and mobile phone messaging made a huge difference to me. I really missed regular catch ups with friends when Catherine was ill and in hospital, life was just so busy and stressful. But thanks to my Facebooking friends, and those who used texting and messaging apps, I was able to keep in touch with everyone. It was hugely positive, it meant I felt supported and a little less alone in my worries. It's also fascinating to see how many people are around in the middle of the night! Friends would post comments in the early hours of the morning; those in healthcare working a night shift, and some in other countries who are in a different time zone, other carers who were awake doing a similar thing to me, or just insomniacs! I always showed everyone's messages to Tony who isn't on social media but enjoys reading the comments. We really appreciated the concern and kind messages from our online family and friends. They honestly kept me going through many of Catherine's hospital admissions and difficult periods of her life.

Being a social girl, Catherine enjoyed being with family and friends, so we would hold a birthday party for her each year. These were such fun and an opportunity for us to thank people who were supportive to us as well as giving Catherine an opportunity to be centre of attention. We loved a chance to spoil her! I would always buy her a new outfit for the party and encouraged people to gift her clothes as birthday presents, she was notoriously difficult to buy for and bright clothes in lovely fabrics always went down well. I was extremely particular about how Catherine looked, she had so much to cope with as far as her health was concerned I thought making sure she always looked nice was the least I could do for her. She owned more designer clothes than she could possibly wear! Her bright Christmas jumpers always caused people to comment, she loved having people making a fuss over her.

Her birthday, being at the start of September, was almost always in sunny weather and we would have a garden party for family and friends. Her last, and 14th birthday party, was no exception, although this was a smaller gathering as Catherine was less well, we were outside in the garden in the most beautiful sunshine surrounded by friends. It was her perfect day.

13

CARERS

I could write a whole book just on carers! There are people who are so very caring, reliable and go the extra mile, clearly love their job and get enjoyment from looking after others and then there are those who are the opposite (we used to call them the "don't carers").

We started to have carers when Catherine was very young. I found our morning routine almost impossible. Catherine slept so badly and before she had her fundoplication operation, she was sick regularly, producing mountains of washing (bedding and her pj's) and I used to have to get up to her 8 or 9 times a night. The mornings were such a rush of getting meds ready, washing syringes and tubes for her NG and little pots of puree for her feeds, I could not be with both children getting ready to leave the house, have my shower and be ready for work at the same time. We had a neighbour with children the same ages as ours, who worked for a Care Agency, she suggested I should arrange to have care at home. Brilliant idea! Even though I worked in healthcare, this had not occurred to me! Actually, I wasn't really aware that there were agencies that supported disabled children (there aren't many) or that this was something you could organise and pay for yourself without having an official assessment. Her agency was exactly what we needed. I paid to have a cleaner once a week and help each weekday morning to get Catherine up and dressed. It made such a difference, we still rushed because you cannot ever stop the last-minute emergencies, but now there was someone ready to help.

Carers really do see the best and the worst of you, there is no hiding when someone comes into your house first thing in the morning! Of course, it is a stressful time in anyone's house, but the chaos in Catherine's bedroom (piles of bedding and sicked-on clothes) and kitchen (milk bottles, syringes and tubes) from the night before was something to behold! I couldn't really leave Catherine alone whilst I was in the bathroom as she was sicker in the mornings, and therefore at risk of choking, so the carer needed to be someone who could get her up and intervene if necessary whilst I was not immediately to hand.

Most of the carers we had when Catherine was little were really lovely, but one actually said to me "we'd all like to have help getting our children up in the morning wouldn't we"?! No definitely not, having carers in your house is not something any parent would do through choice, especially not one who is so judgemental.

One of the most helpful people was the teenage daughter of some friends of ours. She offered to look after Catherine, at the time she was working as a Care Assistant in Basingstoke Hospital and is one of those people who I described at the beginning of this chapter, a natural carer, just an amazingly kind, caring, helpful person. For her young years she had all the attributes I would look for in someone I was about to trust with my most precious family. She was keen and quick to learn Catherine's feeding routine and medication and was happy to babysit for us to go out in the evening. She would look after Thomas too, which I know some agencies will not do, they will only accept responsibility for the disabled child, and you must arrange separate care for your other children. This young friend would not only offer to look after both children, she positively enjoyed it. She had such a unique connection with both children too, we were so grateful for her help.

I cancelled the morning care for a while as I went through phases where I felt I should be doing all Catherine's care myself, plus she was in hospital so often I was always having to remember to let the care agency know not to come. However, the lack of sleep started to build up again and once Catherine had a gastrostomy for all her feeds and medication, I had bigger mountains of syringes and tubes to wash in the morning from her overnight interventions before I could even start to set up pump feeds for the day. Once she had had her MRI brain scan and we had a diagnosis of sorts, this seemed to open doors. We were allocated a Social Worker where before I know it was thought that I was exaggerating how difficult life was. Surely Catherine was just a small baby who did not feed well? And it must be her manipulating us that she did not sleep. You must have proof that your child has disabilities to get support.

After our Social Worker assessment, we had a care plan put in place. Mainly I managed with help only on weekday mornings. I enjoyed getting Catherine up on Saturday and Sunday, we would have the radio on and sing along, and our routine on a Saturday morning included her having pamper time, with a bubble bath using lovely toiletries.

Towards the end of her life her care became much more medical. It was now impossible to do all her morning cares as they included a couple of nebulisers which would take 15 mins or so, suctioning of her naso-pharyngeal airway, use of oxygen, gastrostomy feeds and meds as well as the usual stuff like pad changes and getting dressed. We were having trouble finding carers who were able to do this kind of specialist intervention, so we had a Continuing Health Care assessment – a 50 page document was completed which detailed every medication, procedure and care given over a 24 hour period. This was supposed to be the answer to our care difficulties. We were successful and the CHC awarded, it was recommended that we had a carer to be present overnight as well as in the morning and evening.

The Agency suggested by the Community Children's Nurse started well, our carer was extremely competent, and her help was really helpful. They employed new carers for our contract to cover the overnight shift but unfortunately these staff did not appear to have any medical training at all. They did not understand most basic use of a suction machine, they began hoisting Catherine whilst still strapped into her wheelchair and attached to her feeding pump, did not set up a nebuliser correctly, and these were just some of the things I saw them do. I did not feel I could trust them with Catherine's interventions and the first review meeting we had was a disaster. Their manager had the most unfortunate manner (putting it politely) and was so rude to our Community Nurse I was quite astounded. That was the end of this care package!

We were left in dire straits, I phoned the local agency who had helped us years ago, and although they were not in a position to do medical interventions, they were very willing to cover general caring stuff like getting Catherine dressed, bathed and pampered, and wash the pile of tubes and syringes. Rescued!

14

SIBLINGS

Thomas and Catherine had a wonderful relationship. From the moment she was born he took to his role as big brother and protector with love, and as a little boy he would always sit next to her, give her toys, push her buggy, and call me if he thought she needed anything, and she responded to him more than anyone else. Everything he did with Catherine, he did through love for her. Just after we came home from neonates, we went to my parents' house, and we attended a function at their local church. I know I am biased but she was a beautiful baby and at this point still only weighed 4lbs or so, so was still premature weight. A friend of Mum's who was in the choir, took at shine to Catherine, and asked to hold her. This was one of the first times we had been out in the world with Catherine since she had been born, and so had not seen people's reactions to our gorgeous tiny baby. She held her for quite a while and took her off to show her to others. Thomas was starting to get anxious, he had not let her out of his sight and after a time he couldn't bear it any longer, rushed over to her and said "you need to give her back now, she's ours"!

We made the decision that we wanted to avoid him feeling that he was a carer, and so tried not to ask him to help with her care, although he was always willing and there were times it was unavoidable as Tony or I needed help and he knew what we were asking for. He always took an interest in everything about her care including her medication and feeding regime. He was once asked in an English literacy lesson at Infant school to write an instruction about something of his choosing. He wrote, and I quote, "If you drink a whole bottle of Triclofos (sedative) you will go to sleep and never wake up. Three mls is all you need for a good night's sleep." Heaven knows what his teacher thought!

He learned how to switch her feeding pump to hold or run when it was left bleeping by a distracted parent, he would lift her from her buggy so she could relax on her bed or armchair or more disturbingly for me would take her to his room to listen to his music – only disturbing because she was not to be found where I had left her and just for a moment I would be really confused at her absence! When we had hoisting installed in our bungalow, he and his friends invented a game where they had to cross the bathroom without touching their feet on the floor, by holding onto the hoist beam and swinging. They were aged around 11 at the time, so well underweight for the limit of the equipment – I just shut the door and went to the other end of the house – you have to pick your battles!

He was able to use her equipment, he could adjust her bed, her buggy, he would remove her travel neck collar when she got home from school (for some reason he never liked her wearing it) and would check her monitors when she was in hospital. One time, my poor Mum was in hospital in London after having a heart attack. I took Thomas with me to visit her in the Coronary Care Unit. When we arrived in her room, he went straight over to her monitor and after checking her readings said "Granny, you are doing very well, your sats are 94% with the oxygen and your heart rate is ok too", the nurse looking after Mum was very amused!

We were at a neighbour's party when he was about 4 (Catherine would have been a year or so) I had laid her on a blanket on the floor, and a small crawling baby came over to investigate. I could see Thomas had spotted this from across the room and was watching closely. The baby leaned over to touch her, and Tom shot across the room and grabbed the pointing finger, he glared at the poor surprised baby and growled "don't touch her, leave her alone"! One terrified baby!

It was always hard for him to see Catherine ill. The hospital appointments when she was young meant Thomas coming too, and when Catherine was very poorly, often weeks on end were spent in hospital. Where possible I tried to find someone to look after him, but over the years he spent many long hours in hospital playrooms or sharing my chair whilst we read together on the ward, after school and at weekends. I know we were blessed that he was such a content child. Many were the times that our plans had to be cancelled as Catherine was ill.

One day I remember having to ring the Day Unit from the beach in Southsea where Catherine was vomiting blood, and rushed both children from our day out with friends to Basingstoke hospital and Thomas was back in the playroom with the box of dinosaurs! Other times we would have to cancel days out or cinema trips, promises of McDonalds and all sorts of other treats because Catherine had been ill during the night or had become ill during the day. He was used to suddenly being scooped up with whatever toy he was playing with, or with his little mouse computer, and coming with me and poorly Catherine to the Assessment Day Unit. I always tried to see our GP rather than using the open access facility, in the hope we would avoid an admission. Sadly this did not work very often, we rarely saw our own GP and the GP doing the clinic, or the triage nurse, would do a sats check, and horrified at the reading would ring the hospital, and off we would be sent back to the children's assessment unit and poor Thomas and Catherine would be back in their usual positions.

Thomas was so familiar with the wards in Basingstoke and Southampton, when we arrived he would just go off to check everything was where he left it in the playroom and come back with the toys he liked best, or would play with the siblings of other regulars on the wards. He knew exactly which dinosaurs were to be found in each of the playrooms at Basingstoke and Southampton, although was very put out if there was another child playing with them. He said once " I prefer it when Catherine is in Southampton Hospital to Basingstoke" I was horrified as Catherine was only ever in Southampton if she was seriously ill, but on questioning him more it transpired he preferred the selection of dinosaurs in Southampton! He could read and write well before he started school which is probably down to the many hours he and I spent together reading at Catherine's bedside.

He coped with all the hours that one of us was absent from home whilst with Catherine at hospital and observed our years of worry and frustration around her care. If he was ever jealous of all the attention she commanded, he certainly never showed it to us.

As they grew and Thomas obviously became more independent, he still would regularly check on Catherine when we were at home, he would talk to her, hold her hand, stroke her hair, adjust her oxygen mask or feeding tube, or just give her a kiss in passing. She would respond with a huge smile.

It is hard to imagine a stronger sibling bond than that between our two children, although I know this applies to other special needs children and their brothers and sisters. Their relationships are unique. They have been brought up in a world where they have had to become adaptable to how everything can change in a heartbeat as their sibling becomes suddenly unwell, they know the worry of whether their sibling will get better and they see them suffer when they are unwell. I know how hard Thomas found it to see Catherine poorly, on machines supporting her and with lines in her arms. We tried to protect him and ensure he had time with friends to have fun away from the stress, but also knowing it was important for them both to see each other at these critical moments. He was so patient whilst she was being cared for and watched our battles to achieve the best for her.

Thomas has assured me that he does not feel he missed out when he was growing up but I know that this has more to do with the fact that he loved Catherine unconditionally, as she did him. He says he does not really remember the time before she was born, and so did not know life to be any different but being a special needs family is not easy and we are proud and grateful that he always looked past her disabilities and had a relationship with her like no other.

15

PROFESSIONALS

Catherine was dependent all her life on help from professionals for her medical, educational and social needs. The number of people involved in her care and the complexity of their intervention grew as she grew. Our confidence and communications skills when dealing with them changed over time as we became more attuned to what we could expect from them and what they needed to know from us. It also became apparent who would do the best for Catherine and who were just ticking their boxes.

Over her life she collected up as many 'ologists and 'icians as you could think of! By the time she started school she was already under 7 consultants as well as her Paediatrician, who were responsible for maintaining her health, or at least their part of it.

We saw her Paediatrician at his school clinic once a term, although it was hoped we could go for a longer period without needing to see him, there was always some new problem which couldn't wait and often it was necessary for us to have a double appointment. He ran this clinic with support from the school nurse who kept him up to date with what was happening with each child. She diplomatically covered for his habit of not reading the notes before seeing us, which she did not seem to mind doing, but which never failed to annoy us. However, there is no doubt that his many contacts with colleagues were helpful when specialist referrals were needed.

Most of Catherine's specialist clinics were very helpful and we felt some, like the joint clinics with the General Surgeon and Gastroenterologist, were very thorough and supportive. We were able to voice our concerns, raise issues and always came out with a plan to follow which we felt we had been included in forming.

For all these appointments though, being in Southampton (either at the General Hospital or the Royal South Hants Hospital) we had to allow at least a half day including the journey there. Luckily it is mostly motorway but then there was the stress of hospital parking, always involving long queues, getting to the clinic room and the consultation itself.

If we were seeing the Orthopaedic consultant, we could add at least 2 hours to this. Most of which extra time was spent in the waiting room, waiting for someone to decide whether Catherine needed an Xray, waiting for the Xray, waiting for the result, then waiting for the consultant to interpret the result. We would finally be shown into a cubicle with the Xray up on the lightbox where we would wait again. The Orthopaedic consultant eventually made an appearance, standing at the door of the cubicle to glance at the image and declare "see you again in 6 months". These X-rays were to check that Catherine's hips were not displaced by her high muscle tone. We did complain once about this mismanagement of time and raised the question of how it can be felt appropriate for Catherine to sit in her wheelchair in a crowded waiting room for hours on end? The result was that we were transferred to a different Consultant! A win for us as the new doctor was so much more engaging and had a special interest in children with cerebral palsy all our appointments with her were helpful, and on time.

When Catherine developed a forward curve in her upper spine (kyphosis) she was referred to a spinal surgeon. We saw him in Southampton and following his examination he arranged for us to come back for Catherine to have a series of X-rays taken which would show her spine from different aspects. This was a difficult appointment as the Xray Department did not have hoisting, and for one of the images Catherine was required to sit up with her back against the Xray plate so the picture could be taken facing her from the front. She was not able to sit without maximum support and the forward curve in her spine prevented her from leaning back against the rigid Xray plate. I needed lift her onto the treatment couch and sit with her (wearing a lead coat) to hold her in position. She was around 10 years old by this time and my lifting her was a tricky manoeuvre.

A week later we had a phone call at home from a different Surgeon who said he was ringing as an emergency. He explained that our own Surgeon was away, so he had looked at Catherine's images and it appeared that her kyphosis was unstable and in danger of damaging her spinal cord. This would have the effect of causing a spinal cord injury. In other words, she would become a paraplegic with no movement below the level of the injury. He recommended urgent surgery to correct the kyphosis. He arranged for us to have an appointment the next week. We attended the appointment with great trepidation as we really did not feel surgery would be the right thing for Catherine, especially with her strong muscle spasms. When we got there, we found our original Spinal Surgeon was back and he said he felt that surgery was not necessary at present. His plan was to monitor her instead, with a view to having a spinal brace fitted to support her spine. Two such opposing views! After answering all our questions, we agreed that the decision not to have surgery was the right one, but this episode will always stay with me. Not least because the urgent phone call telling me of the impending spinal cord injury happened during a coffee morning at home and my horrified friends were witness to how suddenly our happy day was thrown into disarray, highlighting the fragility of Catherine's health.

We were introduced some services I had never even been aware of prior to being Catherine's Mum. One of these was a dentist who specialised in special needs dentistry, she was so caring, and cannily she managed to get Catherine to open her mouth to have her teeth checked without losing any fingers! This didn't alter the fact that poor Catherine had to have 6 of her baby teeth removed as they didn't come out when her adult teeth came through. The operation had to be done in hospital as a day case, under anesthetic, and remains in my memory as one of the most horrible experiences for her. How do you console a child who wakes up retching, with a mouth full of bloody swabs after having 6 teeth removed but does not understand any of it? We were the last people to leave the day unit as it took Catherine hours to settle well enough to go home. The place was in darkness by the time we left and the last, very patient, concerned nurse saw us out. I know she was worried about how Catherine would be at home but with regular pain relief she slept some of that night and slowly recovered. Rather than money for her 6 missing teeth, the tooth fairy bought her some pretty fairy lights for her bedroom! Thankfully our appointments with the special dentist following this were just for check-ups. The other thing which was agreeable about this dentist was that she was based in a building which was on the ground floor with parking immediately outside. How lovely!

Contrast to this is our local medical centre. It is in a fairly new premises on the 2nd floor of a building in our town centre. There is an underground car park and the surgery is only accessible via a lift to the ground floor, a walk round through corridors, past a pharmacy to a second lift to the upper floor. As I have mentioned before, our GP was supportive and had known us since Thomas was born so I had no desire to change surgery but our frequent appointments were always a challenge with Catherine in her wheelchair.

I could not write this book without including the contribution of all the many nurses who helped support us throughout Catherine's life. From her early days in Neonates through to her last days at Naomi House, Firvale respite centre, and the Children's ward in Basingstoke Hospital, we were reliant on the caring, expertise and communication of these vital professionals. I have so many stories involving their kindness, from our various admissions, procedures and interventions throughout Catherine's life that it is difficult to decide which to tell. They were so kind and caring to all of us, not only Catherine.

From that first admission to the children's ward when she was so poorly over the millennium, we were very aware of the need to be Catherine's advocates, to speak for her and make sure everyone understood her vulnerabilities. It was so good to become known to the nursing teams, but really of course, a team is made up of individuals and it was always a relief to see another friendly face when each nursing shift changed. They knew us as a family as well as Catherine's individual care needs.

I remember one occasion when Catherine was little she had been very sick, she had a temperature, was wheezy and retching so much she was not coping with her feed, she was inconsolably distressed. Her condition had worsened during late afternoon and now it was evening, well after the day unit had closed. We were desperate so we rang the ward to ask for advice, they told us to bring her straight in. Luckily the drive to the hospital was quick as there wasn't much evening traffic and I parked in the disabled bays many of which were free, unusual during the day. I ran with Catherine in her buggy from the car to the lift and from the lift to the ward. One of the nurses was waiting by the door, she told me she had heard Catherine crying as soon as we got out of the lift (this was in the days before there were lockable doors at the end of the ward) and they had a bed ready to admit her. It was such a relief to see a familiar friendly nurse and know that we were now in safe hands. She settled Catherine in, gave her oxygen and the doctor was on his way to come and see her. I know that without trusting us to know when Catherine was very poorly, they would not have taken the risk of admitting her directly onto the ward.

On a couple of occasions when Catherine had been in hospital a while but was improving enough to sit out, the nurse looking after her hoisted her into her wheelchair and took her to the nurses' station to keep an eye on her. Catherine loved this, she was happiest when she was included and no doubt enjoyed all the discussion and banter with the team. If only she could have told me their stories!

Sadly though there were also times when we absolutely despaired of Catherine's care. We made the decision that she should not be alone at all when in Southampton hospital after an occasion when her care was so neglectful it still makes my blood boil remembering it today. Catherine was on the surgical ward after having a procedure and I needed to come home for the night because I was attending an important appointment in Basingstoke the next day. I had made sure I explained to the nurses that she regularly needed wind released through her gastrostomy and to move her position on the bed to stop her skin from getting sore (either side lying or laying on her back). She also had to have the dressing on her gastrostomy button changed every day as her skin was so liable to break down. I wrote all this down on a note which I left on the table next to her bed. I left all the tubes for winding and dressings for her button and told them exactly when I would be back (lunchtime the next day).

When I arrived back her bed was in a state of disarray and her legs were tangled in the sheet, her head was buried under a pillow which she had no way of freeing herself from, her face was puce and she gasped when I removed the pillow. Her gastrostomy site had leaked and was red and sore, the dressing was the same one I had put on her the previous day and was now soaked with smelly exudate (the packet I had left was still in the same position on her bedside table). Catherine was easy to overlook as she did not demand attention and very rarely cried, although they would not have heard anyway with her head under a pillow. I was furious, upset and astounded that they thought so little about such a vulnerable child who was in a side room on her own with no way of calling for help. I wonder whether anyone had even been in the room since I had left her the night before.

One or other of us stayed with her after this which may seem obvious, but when Tom was little it meant him coming too, although he could not have stayed the night with us in hospital, Tony had to come and collect him. Or when he was older, leaving him to see himself to and from school, coming home to an empty house until Tony got back in the evening. Neither of which seemed right over so many years. What would have happened to Tony's business if he'd had to abandon it to become a carer – he was providing for our family.

I know of families who have grandparents involved with childcare or relatives who can help with laundry, cooking, shopping and other household stuff. We did not have any relatives locally and although our friends were great, it is a big ask when faced with years and years of repeated hospital admissions. People used to tell me not to worry about the housework, it'll keep.

What, for 14 years?! We coped as best we could but it was exhausting to be living such unpredictable lives.

Usually though it was a relief when Catherine was admitted to hospital. A strange statement but when she was unwell, she could become very unwell very quickly. We would try everything, but eventually reach the stage where she was so distressed and we were so exhausted we knew we needed professional help. When she was poorly, she often spiked a temperature and did not tolerate her feed, she could cough herself sick.

Her body responded to these regular infections with increased muscle tone making her very difficult to console by cuddling, as she became rigid and desperate, arching her back and straightening her legs. We would try all the most basic things like giving paracetamol, changing her position, removing wind from her tummy, check her pad, stroke her hair and hold her hand. When all this failed we moved onto every available medication or nebuliser until it slowly became clear that she needed professional attention and the next level of care. It was so reassuring to be admitted onto the ward and reunited with staff who knew us and Catherine so well and could prescribe the right treatment.

Obviously I am biased but some of my favourite professionals were the therapists! When Catherine was in hospital, the days and hours were long, she was generally very unwell so it was a real a highlight was when the physios appeared. They were always so positive and encouraging, they moved her limbs and change her position to keep her comfortable and her joints mobile. If she was unwell with a chest infection (often) they performed daily chest physio to help move her secretions and encourage her to cough. Usually this was done by rhythmically patting her chest, side and back, which, once she had got over being rudely awakened, she seemed to enjoy. She was issued with the most astonishing bit of kit, a "shaky vest". This consisted of a waistcoat type affair was velcro-ed round her upper body and attached by tubing to a vibration pump, which was then switched on to give her chest rapid shakes. She laughed at this every time! When she was too unwell to cope with it they just did gentle movements of her limbs, hands and feet. We both enjoyed seeing the physios.

When not in hospital, her special school had some physio hours allocated, so she always had a programme of exercise and movement, which could be carried out by classroom staff. In fact, the classroom staff had so many skills, they were masters of all. Apart from her physio programme they were adept at letting wind out of her tummy through her gastrostomy, hoisting her into different seating, standing frame or into laying on a mat or bed, changing nappies/pads, their skills were so many and varied and I suspect we only knew a small amount of what they had to do for Catherine during their working day. They obviously still had the curriculum to adapt to teach to our daughter who needed so much extra help.

It is true that most of the professionals involved in Catherine's care will be forever remembered by us. We could not have managed without them but it was interesting to observe the all the different personalities, the different approaches of all those involved, and how we felt so much more connected to some than others.

16

BREATHE

Catherine was 11 when we noticed that she was starting to snore in her sleep. We naively thought this was rather cute, but after a few weeks we realised she was making the same noise when she was awake. The noise became louder over time and it soon became obvious that she was struggling to breathe. We were referred to both respiratory consultant and ENT in Southampton and a series of tests, examinations and overnight sleep assessments were arranged. Following these tests, we were told she had an upper respiratory collapse caused by her poor muscle tone, which meant her airway was obstructed. We were suddenly back in frightening unknown territory where we needed to make decisions which would dramatically affect Catherine's future. At the appointment where we were given these test results, we were also given a brief explanation of possible treatments to bypass or remove the collapse in her airway. All the suggestions seemed to be very drastic, including extensive reconstruction surgery to her soft palate, but none were going to offer a definite solution. Of the suggestions put to us, to assist her breathing, we felt a nasopharyngeal airway (NPA) would be the least invasive & non-surgical alternative. We were discharged from the hospital to go home and await an appointment for the procedure to be done. Feeling shocked we walked back to the car with Catherine and just sat in silence, listening to Catherine's stressed noisy breathing, now knowing the cause but without having the solution available.

After another stay in Southampton, she had the NPA put in and thereafter had a plastic tube permanently in place through her nostril, inside her nose and down through her windpipe past the obstruction in her airway, it had plastic tabs which were taped to her cheeks. The tube needed suctioning to keep it clear and replacing regularly. I hated the look of it and felt so sad that poor Catherine, who did not understand, had to rely on this uncomfortable tube to breathe. The tube almost certainly gave her an extra two years of life.

In June 2013, after a normal Friday at school, Catherine had a cold which seemed to worsen quickly that evening. I rushed her in the car to Basingstoke hospital, once again to Charlie's Day Unit where, despite all the usual treatment (nebulisers, oxygen etc) her condition continued to deteriorate. I called Tony to join us after the on-call Paediatrician had told me off for not calling an ambulance, which would have meant we would come through Emergency Department Resus. I never had done this, I always used our "open access" arrangement to take Catherine myself directly to the Child Health Day Unit as I felt I could get her there as quick as waiting for ambulance. I had completely missed the point that when someone arrives at hospital via ambulance they receive emergency treatment in Resus where they can be stabilised and assessed before being admitted. I had obviously not realised how ill she was, she had been at school a few hours earlier. We were introduced to the on-call Anaesthetist in case her condition should become critical over the weekend.

We have never before had reason to doubt any of the medical advice we had been given about Catherine until that point.

The Anaesthetist took us down the corridor to an area which contained a table behind which he sat, with Catherine's thick file of medical notes in front of him, put his hand on the notes and said "I have seen children like this before, they do not do well after being intubated. I may have to ventilate her, but this will mean having to paralyse her which she may not survive. I would then have to pass a tube down into her lungs which she may not survive. We would then have to go by emergency ambulance to Southampton which she may not survive. If she breathes again for herself, we will have to take her off the support and she may not survive that. You will have to make a decision about switching off her ventilator breathing machine". If her condition should deteriorate, he told us he did not feel it would be in her best interests to be ventilated and we should let her die.

I can honestly say we had never been spoken to in such an uncaring way by any of the doctors (although Catherine's Orthopaedic Surgeon came a close second!) We were dumbstruck and furious in equal amounts.

We felt this was a very premature discussion she had not required any hospital admissions since the NP Airway went in a year ago and had we explained to him that she had been at school that day. He was telling us to give up on her, he made a judgement without knowing anything about her, or her quality of life, or us. In fact, Tony had come up in the hospital lift with him, not knowing who he was, and had walked down the corridor behind him. He watched him as he hesitated at the door to Catherine's cubicle and looked at her from several feet away, approached her for a few seconds, before going to find the Paediatrician who had called him up. We felt he had seen Catherine in her seating system, with feeding pump and airway, he saw she had profound learning difficulties and he had written her off.

We could not believe what he was saying to us - who was this man who had decided her life was not worth saving? If there was a chance for her to live, what parent would not choose to take that chance? We were extremely upset and afterwards, in discussion with the on-call Paediatrician (who we knew very well) we said we wanted all treatment for Catherine. She explained that if the Anaesthetist felt she was too much of a risk he would be able to refuse to intubate her. On this occasion, she was admitted to the High Dependency Unit but due to her struggle to breathe and poor fit of her oxygen mask, the on-call Paediatrician had contacted a company to trial a system that was new at the time (Highflow breathing machine). We arranged for a Priest to come and administer the last rights for her. Although she was still struggling and had not slept for 2 days, she was stable for now.

It was heart-breaking to see her struggle and become more and more tired. Still in High Dependency, having been awake and stressed since Friday evening, it was a great relief that Catherine finally fell asleep on Sunday evening. We hoped this was the start of her road to recovery. Tony was with her the following morning, she appeared to be deeply asleep, when the same Paediatrician who had been present the previous occasion, came into the room with a visiting Snr Registrar from PICU in Southampton.

They had come to see the Highflow machine. They both looked at the monitors and then each other and Tony saw the shock on their faces. Catherine's blood pressure was at a dangerous level (high systolic and low diastolic) and her heart rate was critically low. The doctor from Southampton explained quickly to Tony what was happening. It was that moment that I arrived back on the ward. I had been home to have a shower and see Tom, I could see the room full of doctors and assumed I was just in time for the ward round. The cold realisation that I had stepped into a full emergency hit me and we were suddenly being asked whether we wanted Catherine to be resuscitated – she was not asleep, she was dying.

My brain would not compute. I could not think clearly about what was being said to me. I just remember Tony suddenly said, "DO IT". The confident visiting Snr Reg from Southampton was already busy managing the situation and leading the clinicians in the room. I have no memory of exactly what order everything happened. I just remember the chilling sound of medical staff bleeps going off delivering the message "cardiac arrest G2, cardiac arrest G2". Having worked in the acute hospital environment for so much of my career I was used to the alarming adrenalin rush this announcement caused, but this time it was for our daughter. People and machinery appeared. The room filled. We were whisked away and shown into an empty room opposite. The doors were closed and we were alone. We just held onto each other. How had this happened so suddenly, apparently without any warning? How hadn't the monitors picked up the fact that Catherine was critically ill?

We were checked on by the nurses, offered drinks; we paced, sat and paced again, after an hour and a half our doctor came in. He told us they had resuscitated Catherine and she was now ventilated. He had called the Retrieval Team from Southampton to bring their specialist ambulance and team ready to transfer her to Southampton General PICU but he explained that she was not stable enough to be moved yet. We were still not out of the woods.

The Retrieval Team arrived, and Catherine was finally considered stable enough to travel four hours after her cardiac arrest. She was secured to a stretcher and transferred onto mobile 02, ventilator and syringe driver. We were grateful for the professionalism of the paramedic retrieval team and this time one of us was allowed to travel in the ambulance with her. I was given a seat with my back to the driver and facing the rear of the ambulance. Catherine was in front of me, secure on the stretcher unconscious and intubated. All the ventilation equipment, monitors, oxygen and syringe driver were fixed onto the stretcher. As well as the driver there were two paramedics in the back with me and Catherine.

I still remember that journey so clearly, I was in shock, only a few short hours earlier we had been feeling so relieved that Catherine appeared to be sleeping and settled in High Dependency, we thought she was starting to improve. I sat in the ambulance just staring at the top of her head in front of me, which I could just reach to stroke her hair, in disbelief at how her life could have changed so drastically in such a short time.

We left Basingstoke Hospital at 4.30pm and headed straight into the rush hour traffic heading for the motorway. It is a wonder how three lanes of solid traffic leading to the busiest roundabout in Basingstoke can part to allow through an ambulance. The motorway was crowded but we were not delayed or slowed, the traffic just parted to let us through. The paramedics were so professional, confident and efficient, I had total faith in their ability to look after their precious cargo and to keep me informed all through the journey. Although I have to say that I think they seemed to visibly relax when they realised I was not going to have a melt-down in the ambulance, or behave unpredictably! - they probably did not realise how many emergencies we have been involved in, and although this definitely does not make the situation any easier, it does mean you understand a little more about the process.

Before we left the hospital, I had been told that the ambulance would stop if there was any change in Catherine's condition or any concerns about the machines. Just after getting onto the motorway the paramedic in charge alerted to the driver to ask him to stop. We pulled over to the hard shoulder and both paramedics, with their backs to me, were focussed on unconscious Catherine, neither spoke. They were checking her and their monitors. It transpired that one of her heart leads had become dislodged, so was easily fixed, but that moment was up there with one of the most frightening times of my life. We arrived safely in Southampton and were taken through their ED and up in the lift to PICU. We were on our way to safety.

I know we would never have been able to forgive ourselves or move past allowing her to die because we had been pressurised by an on-call Anaesthetist who we had never met before and who thought it appropriate to make his own uninformed judgements. He did not know Catherine, her history, her family situation and did not feel the need to engage us in discussion. This was a decision being made by someone who is not used to being challenged or being asked to justify himself. We cannot imagine a more total abuse of position and lack of caring for his patient. He did not recognise any need to understand or consult with any of the many professionals who had been looking after Catherine her whole life. How can he have thought a few seconds observation from the other side of the room gave him a right to decide whether she should live or die?

The doctor who had led her resuscitation in Basingstoke came to see us once we were settled in PICU, and if he was concerned about our disagreement with the Anaesthetist regarding the rights or wrongs of trying to save her, he certainly did not show it. In fact, he told us that while we were having the situation explained, and being asked our wishes, he was already injecting adrenaline into Catherine's foot. He knew vital seconds could not be wasted. As a Senior Registrar (now Consultant) in Critical Care Child Health I know he was used to treating children with complex needs like Catherine and understood exactly what was needed at that point, which was treatment, not discussion. Without his quick actions, Catherine would have died that day.

Once on PICU, she remained ventilated and stable for 48 hours. It was agreed that they would try to wean her off the ventilator but the ICU consultant explained it was likely that she would not be able to breathe for herself again, that she may not survive, and if she did she may be further brain damaged and wouldn't be the Catherine we knew. I do not remember ever feeling so sad.

The time had come to trial a reduction in ventilator pressures. The machine display showed a red graph line going up and down evenly spaced peaks, a constantly moving marker blipped along the line. It was explained that as the pressures were reduced, Catherine should start to breathe for herself. If she breathed for herself the colour of the peaks on the machine would change from red to green. I found I was holding my own breath as I watched the monotonous red line moving along the peaks and troughs on the screen … then a tiny green dot appeared at the top of one peak; then another dot on the next peak. The green dots grew to green peaks and Catherine was starting to breathe for herself!

I said she was made of strong stuff! She continued to breathe more and more for herself and gradually recovered enough to be taken off the ventilator. She remained on oxygen therapy for a while and once stable she was transferred by ambulance back to Basingstoke for a couple of days, then to Naomi House for 2 nights step-down before coming home. She went back to school about 2 weeks later, smiling and happy. The only outward sign of what she had been through were her very bloodshot eyes and her sore throat. We are so proud of her, that not only did she recover, but she was most definitely back to being our lovely Catherine.

After this horrendous episode and when Catherine was back home and well, we completed a purple form. A purple form is a document known as an Advanced Care Plan (now reSPECT*) which details a person's wishes for care to be given, or not given, in the event of a cardiac arrest or other medically life-threatening situation. In the case of a child with complex or life-threatening illness, those with parental responsibility are involved in discussions with the child, if applicable, and their medical team, to make these decisions.

We were deeply troubled by the events around Catherine's cardiac arrest when we felt we were being pushed to make decisions we were not ready to make and this was in an emergency situation when it is so hard to think clearly. These are discussions that should happen as part of a person's care plan and not with clinicians who do not know the patient or their family. We discussed our feelings with our Paediatrician who arranged for us to have a purple form to complete. It was easy! We were both in no doubt we wanted all care to be given even should a similar event happen again, although this episode had shown us just how vulnerable Catherine had now become and we were aware that the next time could be equally life threatening.

We had a lovely summer. Amazingly the weather was the best we had had for many years and we were able to be in the garden, out for walks and went to our holiday home on the Isle of Wight. All of these are Catherine's favourite things. She celebrated her 14th birthday on 2nd September 2013 in our garden in the sunshine with her friends.

Catherine went back to school in September and loved to see all her friends again.

At the beginning of October, the inevitable happened and she caught a cold. She was back in Basingstoke Hospital again and for two weeks struggling with low oxygen levels and poorly tummy. She had a sudden deterioration, and the decision was made to ventilate again and again she was transferred to Southampton PICU.

Another trip in a blue light ambulance - this is one of those most terrifying of experiences that would never become any easier. I have described Catherine's first trip in an ambulance when she was a baby, and we were not allowed to travel with her. She had many trips to Southampton General since that time, but these were planned, blue light ambulance trips are a whole different experience. Again, the Retrieval Team came from Southampton and prepared her to travel and again I was able to travel with her but this time we had an "ambulance chaser" following us. This is a term I had not heard before but is the name given by the paramedics to someone who decides that following in the wake of an ambulance which is travelling at full speed is a good way to beat the traffic. As we all know, the traffic parts to let an ambulance through and if a car is following behind people often assume the car is part of the emergency but this is not the case and is the most dangerous thing to do. If the ambulance needs to slow or stop for any reason the car following will plough into the back. This particular car followed us for most of the journey. By the time we were driving through Winchester he had been reported to the local police who would find his home address and planned to be waiting on his drive for him to arrive home.

Once Catherine was settled in the Intensive Care Unit the lead Paramedic came to see how she was and was delighted to let us know that the ambulance chaser had been caught and given a fine and points on his license.

During this episode we were introduced to the Palliative Care Team at Southampton. Catherine had been transferred to High Dependency from Intensive Care as although she was not needing full ventilation, she was permanently on breathing support (BiPAP) and unconscious. The doctors could not find any treatable cause for her condition. She had a brain scan (EEG) which showed nothing abnormal and their other tests were equally inconclusive. We were told her current unconscious state was likely to be due to her systems failing under the stress of her respiratory collapse and increasingly poor muscle tone, and her prognosis was extremely poor.

Distressingly, there was a large graph at the end of her bed with "Coma Scale" written on it and her regular checks were being plotted along lines which made grim reading. An appointment was made for us to meet with the Palliative Care Consultant the following week. In true Catherine-style, she had different ideas and over the weekend she began to wake up. The first signs we saw were a tiny movement at the side of her mouth, which turned into a small twitch of a smile. By Monday morning she was propped up in bed wearing a Christmas Tshirt smiling round at everyone! Our meeting with the Palliative Care Consultant was helpful, we were to be transferred home via Naomi House where we would make end of life plans, although thankfully it seemed these were not needed just yet.

17

LAST MONTHS

Catherine's last few months were really hard for her but also for us, Thomas (now aged 17) was approaching his A Level finals at 6th Form college and Catherine needed to have one of us either with her or near all the time. I think the term rollercoaster is overused but does give the correct image of our lives hurtling along a track over which we had no control and involved a few good spells when our hopes would be raised, only to then come crashing down.

I really struggled with work during this time, I was all over the place. I made poor decisions and forgot important information given to me by my patients. I remember doing an assessment for a lady who was needing a specific type of wheelchair, involving the most straightforward of decision on my part but when I came to write up the assessment and prescription for equipment, my mind was blank.

I wish I had had the foresight to know that I needed to stop working and be with Catherine. That is such a difficult call though, knowing exactly what "approaching end of life" means, is this months, weeks or days? I knew I needed to make a decision after a night where I had been with Catherine in hospital until the early hours of the morning, managed a few hours' sleep at home and then had to be back for the ward round at 9am. I arrived late to work and realized I would never be able to make up the hours I was needing to take off. Unfortunately, at that time our manager worked on a different site (actually in the New Forest, so far away we never saw him). I didn't have the energy to fight the system so I continued working through her last weeks. I am ever indebted to my OT colleagues who stepped in on a couple of occasions to see my wheelchair clinic patients for me.

Catherine survived more hospital admissions that last Autumn, but all were emergency admissions via Resus and ended in HDU. We still generally spent our nights at home when Catherine was an inpatient as we were so sleep deprived this was the only way to get through the days but we dreaded the phone ringing in the middle of the night from respite, hospital ward or Naomi House to say that Catherine was seriously unwell again. Each time she recovered less well and by December we amended our end of life wishes for her. During an admission to Naomi House their Consultant helped us with these huge decisions, we accepted the fact that she would not survive the trauma of another intubation. With his help we wrote a new advanced care plan.

Although these discussions were difficult for us, the Hospice Consultant had a wonderful, clear way of explaining things, with total sensitivity, and it was definitely a two-way discussion – watch and learn Mr Anaesthetist! He was endlessly patient and gave us all the time we needed to ask questions. It was clear that Catherine's Cerebral Palsy was causing her low muscle tone to no longer support her breathing and her airway collapse was now affecting her whole respiratory system including her lungs. Although she had always had a strong cough, she could not clear the secretions from her lungs quickly enough, and her airways were struggling to cope with the volume of fluid she was producing.

Her last few weeks were excruciating for her and it was painful for us to see her in pain. We had been told many times by now that she was effectively "end of life", but Catherine continued to be strong. She would wake a few times a day for 20 minutes or so when she would be cheerful but exhausted. She had been on course after course of antibiotics which were no longer preventing the infection in her lungs and they were now affecting her bowels. Her constant pad changes and abdominal cramps were painful for her and in turn meant she was not coping with her feed. We suggested to our families and close friends that they might want to come and see her as soon as possible. We were so pleased that they did, everyone who came saw her awake and smiling during this time.

I used to lie awake and agonise about how it would be when she finally did not recover, I lived in fear, and in fact there were times where I just felt chilled to the bone, cold and shivering. By now she was obviously tired and weak; she constantly had an upset tummy and needed a bipap non-invasive ventilator to support her breathing, but so far, only at night. I had learned how to use this and we had our own machine at home. She was too poorly to go out of the house, so one of us would go to work, while the other would be at home with Catherine. She was requiring constant intervention from one or both of us through both the day and night.

By mid-December Catherine was at Naomi House after another hospital discharge and was not well for long enough to come home. The Naomi House team supported us through this painful time when we were struggling to get through each day not knowing what would happen. Their positive attitude and outlook meant that when she was well enough, they would do gentle activities and include her in whatever was happening even if it was only in some small way and they would encourage and support us.

I know we would not have coped at the end of Catherine's life had it not been Christmas & New Year, and that Tony and I were both able to take time off work. Tony, Tom and I were all feeling unwell, probably partly due to our stress levels but also due to the usual winter bugs and chest infections.

I brought Catherine home from Naomi House on Christmas Eve, and it felt so magical to have her back with us at home. We set up the bipap machine and her oxygen, as well as all the usual feed, medicine and nebulisers. Between us we managed to get an hour or so sleep at a time at night around being woken by the bipap which was bleeping often with lack of seal round her face. Yes, it is infuriating to lose sleep to equipment failures when your sleeping child is settled and comfortable.

There were moments in the middle of the night or early hours of the morning when I had finished doing some sort of intervention for Catherine and the house was quiet, I would hold her, gazing at her, breathing in her scent and trying to consciously create an image of her to keep in my memory.

Tony's sister and her husband travelled to us on Christmas Day, it was such a relief to see them. Cheerful people with their minds set on helping, and they arrived with an entire Christmas dinner - turkey, pudding and all the trimmings! We had arranged for a carer to come on Christmas morning to make a fuss of Catherine, she got her up, dressed and pampered. With their help and support we had a lovely Christmas. I can only think how different our memories would have been of that last Christmas had they not been so generously prepared to share their time and energy with us. They were bright, happy and fun and of course made a fuss of Thomas and Catherine. We made sure we took plenty of photos during the few hours that Catherine was awake and smiley and responsive, but by now she was on high levels of breathing support and she slept for most of the time.

She went back to Naomi House for a couple of days between Christmas and New Year and came home again for New Year.

Tony was trying to work from home on Friday 3rd January, but by this time looking after Catherine was a full-time effort. I worked until 2pm and when I got home Tony said how worried he was that Catherine was having difficulty breathing. He had been repositioning her, suctioning and had worked through all the medication available but nothing was helping. He was not able to calm her down by holding her as she was so distressed. I had arranged for two of her special needs friends to come visit just for a short while, but it was clear Catherine was really struggling to breathe. None of her medication or nebulisers made any difference, nothing we tried helped, and she could not tolerate the bipap. We knew we had reached the end of what we could do for her.

We called an ambulance which thankfully arrived within minutes as it had been rerouted from another call. The concern of the Paramedics was obvious, they were quick and efficient, they cut her oxygen mask off to replace with their portable supply and transferred her to a stretcher, and into the ambulance.

I went in the ambulance with them. Although we live only a mile or so from Basingstoke Hospital, this felt a long journey. Catherine was distressed, she actually looked terrified, heaving with her whole body trying to gasp enough oxygen into her lungs to breathe. The Paramedic in the back with us was constantly communicating with the driver. We were taken quickly into resus where we spent several hours whilst the team were working with her, poor Catherine was fighting with her whole chest and abdomen to try and catch her breath.

Maybe it is just coincidence, but Catherine's own Paediatrician was on duty, as was the Head of Child Health, who had known us since she was Ward Sister when Catherine had her first admission as a baby. Tony and I had previously decided there should have no more cannulae inserted (due to the years of trauma to her veins this was always a difficult procedure) but we could not watch her struggle like this. We agreed one attempt but no more, her lovely Consultant managed to do this with one go and she was then able to have medication in this way. They eventually managed to stabilise her, and she was transferred to the Children's Ward about midnight. After discussion and a phone call, it was arranged for her to be moved in the morning back to Naomi House where she would stay until the end of her life. At 1.00 am, exhausted and feeling unwell, we went home for a few hours' sleep, a decision I will regret for the rest of my life.

Although she remained stable and in a deep sleep overnight, she suddenly deteriorated in the morning. We had planned to return to the hospital first thing, but we had that dreaded phone call from the Ward telling us to come quickly, Catherine's breathing had changed. We were as quick as we could be but the three of us arrived on the ward 5 minutes too late. She died that morning still in hospital. It was 4th January; she was aged 14.

Although our preferred place of death was Naomi House (yes, that is a thing – it is one of the decisions we had made during advanced care plan discussions), we were ok with the reality that she was too unwell to move and we felt we were among friends at Basingstoke Hospital. Many of the doctors, nurses and other staff had known Catherine, and us, all her life and we were really moved to see how many people came into her room to say goodbye. There was a little knock on the door and one of the nurses told us she was going off shift and wanted to say goodbye, she came in, obviously upset. She said, "there's a queue of people outside who want to come and pay their respects". The nurses from the night shift were leaving and morning shift was just starting, they came in to see us one at a time. This meant so much to us. Despite being in shock and so numb this is one of the things I still remember clearly.

Her causes of death were respiratory collapse, pneumonia and cerebral palsy. Her continuing healthcare package with a new agency had been due to start that night.

We were asked whether we would still like Catherine to be transferred to Naomi House. This may seem a strange question for anyone who has not had experience of children's hospice services, but I was horrified at the thought of her body being taken to the hospital morgue. I had always been clear that I did not want this to happen. So, it was arranged for her to be transferred to the Naomi House Butterfly Suite (I would describe this as a nondenominational chapel of rest).

Unfortunately, the reality is that if someone dies in hospital they are required to leave through the morgue. Catherine was to be moved from the Children's Ward, down to the Undertaker's car which would take her to Naomi House. She was laid on her side on the bed with a teddy obscuring her face. The three of us accompanied her with one of the nurses (who knew us well) down in the lift and through the morgue. Here Tony lifted her for the last time off her bed, onto the undertaker's gurney and out into a waiting hearse. Her body was transferred to Naomi House and our family were encircled into their care.

We remained in the Butterfly Suite for a few days before her funeral was arranged. Catherine was placed on a cooled bed in a cooled room which was beautifully and peacefully decorated, with a separate lounge for family. It is hard to describe how important that time was, Naomi House with their specialism and expertise nurtured us and helped us with all that needed to be done for Catherine's funeral. This is difficult enough at any time, but just after Christmas and New Year bank holidays, it was even more challenging. During this period when we were so raw with grief, it was hard to make decisions, and they were there to guide us. They also helped with memory making, we have hand and footprints and locks of Catherine's hair tied with ribbon. It allowed time for visits by some of our friends, and staff from Catherine's school, to say goodbye.

The funeral was well attended, the service was full and many of the people who came saw a double rainbow over the church which contained Catherine and everyone who loved her.

18

BEYOND

To say that losing Catherine left a huge hole in our lives does not come close to describing the enormity of how everything changed for us when she died. It felt as though a bomb had exploded and everything in our lives was shattered. The numb feeling lasted months and I realise I do not remember much about the whole year after she died. The hours we spent caring for her had been gradually increasing over the last two years of her life as her condition was deteriorating, and when she died, those hours were suddenly empty.

We had been seriously worried about her for weeks and barely saw each other as we took turns to care for her, be with her in hospital, work and sleep. We were so busy we didn't have time to speak about much else. We now felt utterly bereft. There is no doubt in my mind that her last weeks were extremely hard for her and I couldn't help but re-live the look of fear in her eyes as she struggled to breathe. These images haunted me.

We did what we needed to do, we shared our tears and our memories, we went for long walks, listened to music and buried ourselves in our work. We missed Catherine and everything about her and felt overwhelmed by the traumatic events we had shared as a family. Our routines had been built around her and her life, suddenly all of it disappeared.

I stopped being Chairman for the School PTA, in fact, my last meeting frightened me, I really struggled to make decisions about the simplest things. We obviously had no more contact with any of Catherine's doctors, nurses, health care workers, teachers, respite staff, and all those people who had been increasingly central to our lives for 14 years. Everything we did had revolved around Catherine's needs and cares, for the whole of her life, and all our relationships with friends and family had gradually changed over that time.

It had been so long since we had been able to have a normal social life, we had no idea how to start.

What even is spare time?! Everything seemed so pointless.

2014 was a very difficult year for our family, Tom had his 18th birthday 2 weeks after Catherine's funeral, we wanted to mark the occasion but there could be no celebration feeling the way we all felt, the three of us went for a quiet meal in a local pub. My loving, gentle Mum died 3 months almost to the day after Catherine, and my brothers and I spent several weekends meeting together in her North London house to dismantle our childhood home ready for sale. Tom took his A levels that summer and did not get the grades he was hoping for to go to his chosen University to study Maths. Although he did go, it was through the University clearing system which was unnecessarily stressful. His going to Uni left Tony and I at home with an unplanned empty nest.

Our friends were hugely supportive, and I know my special needs Mum friends kept an eye on me, they took turns to text me and we arranged to meet up often. We went on spa days, for coffees and lunches. We laughed and cried together, and I know they felt and shared my grief. I am aware that each of them, and in fact many parents of special needs children, have experienced medical emergencies and health crises with their own children and faced the real fear of loss.

In time though, everything settles into a routine and time moves on, and it is then that those meet ups can be more difficult. Although I love to hear how their children (now young adults) are doing, there is always talk of their transition to the next life stage and the usual trials and tribulations of fighting the system that we used to be part of, for me our meetings are sometimes bittersweet. I know how frustrating their ongoing battles are but oh how I miss being part of them. I dreaded meeting new people who might ask whether I have children, the next question would inevitably be "how many"? I have never found the best answer.

Over our years of caring for Catherine it had become very clear to us that there is real lack of understanding about the role of a parent carer. Caring for a disabled child is not the same as childcare and looking after a child with life limited illnesses is all consuming. It is now also clear to us that people equally do not understand that grief is similarly all consuming. The sudden loss of purpose and devastation of our lives alongside the grief of losing our happy little girl will never be left behind. We live constantly with memories of Catherine and her extraordinary life and all the emotions felt over her years. She is in our minds the whole time and every birthday, anniversary, Christmas and New Year is as difficult as the last.

The 2020 Corona virus lockdowns have had the effect of giving us a little extra time as a family to be together and the pressure to be social has been removed. We are all still working but our leisure time is now limited in the same way as everyone else, we do not have to try and redress our work life balance. Tony was working entirely from home for the lockdown periods which may have reduced some of his daily stress, and now divides his work between home and office. He has always been busy with his Practice but now obviously doesn't have to constantly balance his time between his business and family emergencies anymore, he can make plans which do not have to be suddenly cancelled. A sad reality is that since Catherine died we have more time for socialising but less inclination to do so.

After his realisation that a life of Maths was not for him, Tom completed a Software Engineering apprenticeship and is happy working as a Software Programmer.

I have changed my job since Catherine died. I wanted to work more hours but also felt I needed new challenges. I was doing a wheelchair assessment at our local adult hospice in Basingstoke, where Catherine's Godmother was working and where I had known the small team of therapists for a while. I realised this was a role I might enjoy and could give me the change I was looking for. I applied to join the bank for locum OTs, thinking I could do a few hours a week for them. I wanted to make sure I would be able to cope with the role on a personal level before I took the plunge to commit to a permanent change. It took about a week before I knew this was a team I would enjoy working with and in an area where I feel at home.

I have been working there for over 5 years now and find the job hugely rewarding. We are a small team of hospice-based therapists but part of the wider Palliative Care Team which involves working closely with speciality doctors, community and inpatient nurses, Macmillan team and specialist teams.

My role as a palliative care Occupational Therapist includes supporting our inpatient unit where we offer symptom control and end of life care. We are involved in discharge planning for those patients whose wish is to be at home for the end of their life. This includes organising equipment for home, advice on moving and handling, helping find the best routine for the individual and to support the families. We also work in the community doing home assessments, and even in these times of social distancing, our patients are grateful to have face to face advice, equipment and support in their last weeks and days of life. Although we may not be able to change the outcome, we can help improve the quality of last days.

I have the opportunity to use all the OT skills I have accumulated over the years, as well as my own experiences of living with a family member who is seriously ill and equipment dependent. I am pleased that end of life care in the community has improved over recent years, but I can't help thinking how helpful it would have been for our family to have this kind of support with our care of Catherine.

One personally significant thing I have learned through my work in palliative care is that even the most experienced specialist in this field cannot give an exact answer to the most commonly asked question "how long have I got?" I find this oddly reassuring, that there are so many really complicated factors involved in an individual's death, there are no right or wrong decisions, and every family has their own unique dynamic. Also, even the most well thought out plan can be overcome by unpredictable events.

I have taken up hobbies and interests I had not had time to do since Catherine was born. When she was in Paediatric Intensive Care she had been given a beautiful quilt which had a label in one corner that read "made with tender loving care by Project Linus". I had looked this up and discovered Project Linus is an organisation which distributes homemade quilts to poorly children in hospital, and I promised myself that if I ever had time, I would make a quilt to donate back. I have joined a local quilting group and learned how to make quilts, with varying levels of skill, but I have now donated 5 cot quilts to the charity. I have also had time to take up cake decorating again and love to make cakes for people, it is a real privilege when someone asks me to make a cake for their special occasion.

I started as a volunteer for Naomi House Children's Hospice, who were so supportive to us during Catherine's life. I spent a few hours a week working in their Retail offices but then heard about their Ambassador scheme and I have been doing this for 5 years now. I have done a variety of roles as Ambassador, including supporting fundraising events like fun runs and village fetes, promotional events, and I do presentations about Naomi house to organisations large and small. I am very honoured that I was asked to talk about our family's experiences of the Hospice at a social event held on the Terrace at the House of Commons to celebrate their 21st birthday. I love that I get to talk about Catherine and our experiences at the same time as helping raise the profile of what this amazing charity does for families like ours.

I am most proud though that Tony and I have found a way to use some of the extraordinary skills we accumulated over the years we were caring for Catherine. We have become approved Foster Carers and we currently provide weekend specialist respite care to two families who each have a child with severe and profound disabilities. We find this so rewarding, the children are delightful, and we can use the skills we learned through Catherine to support families who are desperately in need of a break from their caring roles. We know exactly how that feels.

It is now 7 years since Catherine's death, and gradually we appear to be finding our way through the grief. We feel that we have found ways to take Catherine with us in our new ventures, which seems to make the heartbreak of missing her a little more bearable. We think about her all the time and talk about her often. Catherine will always be with us and has made us who we are today, we are so proud of our brave beautiful girl.

Footnotes:

* Recommended Summary Plan for Emergency Care and Treatment (ReSPECT) is a process supported by the Resuscitation Council (UK) and UK Royal Colleges to create personalised anticipatory care plans for patients, including wishes and plan for end of life.

** BiPAP is a machine can help push air into the lungs. The patient wears a mask or nasal prongs that are connected to a ventilator. The machine supplies pressurized air through the mouth and/or nose into the airways. It is called "positive pressure ventilation" because the device helps open the lungs with this air pressure.

AFTERWORD

I hope I have fairly represented the reality of caring for a child with ongoing and complex healthcare needs. Catherine's needs came before everything else, there was no alternative. It was this that created a feeling of living in a strange parallel world where there were options, but not for us, our lives were dictated by Catherine's routine and the specialist skills required to meet her needs. That we could not manage without the support and help of all the people mentioned in my book was also a fact and not a choice. But because of this we met people we would never have met, and we had remarkable, extraordinary experiences that changed our perspective of the world.

I wanted to show that this kind of parenting is completely different from bringing up a child who will hopefully grow up and go out in the world to be independent, carve their own path and make their own decisions.

We always felt the monumental challenge of nurturing, advocating and protecting Catherine gave our lives particular meaning. We were blessed that through her our family learned the meaning of unconditional love, our love for Catherine and hers for us.

Tony reminded me recently of the song lyrics "what have you done today to make you feel proud?" we agreed that we had the answer to this every morning when we woke to begin another day of caring for Catherine.

****

ABOUT THE AUTHOR

Val is proud to work for St Michael's Hospice in Basingstoke as a palliative care Occupational Therapist and lives with her husband Tony and son Tom in Basingstoke, Hampshire